Law and Society
Volume 4

Logical Concepts in Legal Positivism
Legal Norms from a Philosophical Perspective

Volume 1
Criminological Theory. Just the Basics
Robert Heiner

Volume 2
Is Legal Reasoning Irrational? An Introduction to the Epistemology of Law
John Woods

Volume 3
The Law's Flaws. Rethinking Trials and Errors?
Larry Laudan

Volume 4
Logical Concepts in Legal Positivism. Legal Norms from a Philosophical Perspective
Juliele Maria Sievers

Law and Society Series Editors
Robert L. Heiner
John Woods

rheiner@plymouth.edu
john.woods@ubc.ca

Logical Concepts in Legal Positivism
Legal Norms from a Philosophical Perspective

Juliele Maria Sievers

© Individual author and College Publications 2016
All rights reserved.

ISBN 978-1-84890-132-9

College Publications
Scientific Director: Dov Gabbay
Managing Director: Jane Spurr

http://www.collegepublications.co.uk

Original cover design by Laraine Welch
Printed by Lightning Source, Milton Keynes, UK

All rights reserved. No part of this publication may be reproduced, stored in a retrieval system or transmitted in any form, or by any means, electronic, mechanical, photocopying, recording or otherwise without prior permission, in writing, from the publisher.

Foreword

The present book offers an original approach on the legal notions developed by Hans Kelsen in his attempts towards a "pure" theory of Law, based on a philosophical analysis of the main legal concepts that have a strong philosophical feature, namely those notions which are somehow "shared" between the two fields in their name, but not always in their meaning. While the most striking notion to be approached via a philosophical perspective would probably be that of *legal validity* (since validity is a central term also in Logic), we aim, in the same way, to approach the notions of *legal fictions*, the notion of *science* in Law, *normative conflicts* or *"contradictions"* as they are commonly – and wrongly – named, and the *rule of inference* as it is applied in the context of normative creation, giving place to the wrong notion of practical reasoning. The notion of practical reasoning is very rich in this context of comparison, and will be a special one, as it serves for us to analyze traditional problems of legal theory, such as Jørgensen's dilemma, as well as it offers us the opportunity of providing our own alternative of a logical treatment of the process of legal justification of the creation of a norm. We aim to rapidly analyze the notion of legal and logical conditions as well, which represent a changing in Kelsen's perspective on the utility and legitimacy of the application of logic to the legal domain.

Such a comparative study, even if it appears to be fundamental for clarifying those notions in their respective fields, is a task never before developed in this systematic manner.

The objective of this book is to provide a clear overview of the boundaries between the fields of philosophy (especially logic) and the legal norms. A clear understanding of the relations between those "homonym" notions may explain why they are most of the time misused when philosophers talk about law, as well as when lawyers try to justify the concepts composing the legal theory.

The context of this study is the legal positivism as it is explained by the legal-philosopher Hans Kelsen. This choice is justified by the fact that Kelsen's legal theory appears to be the most suitable frame for an analytical, logic-oriented investigation. The work emphasized will be the General Theory of Norms (1979), mainly because of the fact that this book represents how intensively Kelsen dedicated himself to the legal problems mostly related to philosophy or logic, namely the question of the application of logic to norms and the clarification of problematic notions such as the basic norm as a fiction or, still, the notion of modally indifferent substrate.

This book is the outcome of several years of research on the topic concerning the approximation between the fields of law and logic. The fruitful environment provided by the Laboratory "Savoir, Textes, Langage" in the University of Lille 3, in France, as well as the Law Department of the University of Konstanz, in Germany, were fundamental for the results achieved. I would like to thank professors Shahid Rahman and Mathias Armgardt for the important comments and corrections to my manuscripts. I also present my gratitude to my colleague Sébastien Magnier: his knowledge in dialogical logic was widely profitable in Chapter 9 of this book. Finally, I would like to thank the Philosophy Department of the *Universidade Federal de Santa Maria*, in Brazil, were I currently am a member of the Post-Graduation Program, as well as the scholarship program PNPD-CAPES, which funds my researches.

Table of Contents

1. Introduction 1
2. **The Author and his Theory** 9
   2.1 Three Schools of Thought, or: Why Legal Positivism? 10
      2.1.1 Legal Realism 11
      2.1.2 Natural Law Theory 13
      2.1.3 Legal Positivism 16
   2.2 Why Kelsen 19
      2.2.1 The Historical Context 19
      2.2.2 The *Pure Theory of Law* (1960 21
      2.2.3 The *General Theory of Norms* (19 23
3. **Preliminary Notions** 28
   3.1 The Notion of Legal Validity 29
      3.1.1 Defining "Legal Norm 30
      3.1.2 Validity as Existence 33
   3.2 Legal Science and its Object: Hume's Naturalistic Fallacy 36
      3.2.1 Hume's Naturalistic Fallacy 37
      3.2.2 The Relations between the Science and its Object 40
   3.3 Legal Conditions 43
      3.3.1 Imperatives and Norms 43
      3.3.2 Causality and Imputation 45

    3.4   Fictions 47

           3.4.1   The Hierarchy of Norms...................................49

           3.4.2   The Basic Norm (*Grundnorm*) 52

    3.5   Normative Conflicts and Logical Contradictions 55

           3.5.1   The Problem of Applicability 56

           3.5.2   Conflicts between Norms 57

           3.5.3   Derogation 59

           3.5.4   Temporality and Efficacy 61

    3.6   Practical Reasoning and the Rule of Inference 63

           3.6.1   Dissipating the Confusion 65

    3.7   Final Remarks on this Topic 66

4.   **Legal Positivism: A Defense of the Scientific Method**........................68

    4.1   Positivism versus Natural Law Theories 69

           4.1.1   Legal Validity and the Positive Law Perspective 75

           4.1.2   Static versus Dynamics 76

           4.1.3   Normative Content and the Natural Law Perspective .81

    4.2   Understanding the Tension 84

    4.3   Overcoming the Tension 86

    4.4   Final Remarks on this Topic 88

5.   **Science and Method: The Naturalistic Fallacy**................................... 92

    5.1   David Hume as a Model 93

           5.1.1   The "Ought" 96

           5.1.2   The "Is" 99

    5.2   One Example of the Fallacy: Jørgensen's Dilemma 101

	5.3 Final Remarks on this Topic 106
6.	**The Non-Existence in Legal Science** 109
	6.1 Legal Science: Meaning and Particularities 110
	6.1.1 Some Examples 112
	6.1.2 Dichotomies in Kelsen's Theory 115
	6.2 The Basic Norm as a Scientific Fiction 116
	6.2.1 The Searching for Justification 117
	6.2.2 Understanding the Fiction 120
	6.2.3 A Little Help from Philosophy 121
	6.3 Where is the Basic Norm? 122
	6.4 Final Remarks on this Topic 126
7.	**Normative Conflicts and Temporality in Law** 128
	7.1 Norms versus Sentences 129
	7.2 Derogation 132
	7.2.1 The Formulation of the Derogation Norm 132
	7.3 The context of the Normative Conflict 134
	7.3.1 Some Examples 135
	7.4 Retroactivity 137
	7.5 The Basic Norm 139
	7.6 Final Remarks on this Topic 141
8.	**The Notion of Practical Reasoning (Part I)** 143
	8.1 Introduction 144
	8.2 Understanding Jørgensen's Dilemma 146
	8.3 First Attempts: Jørgensen and Ross 146

		8.3.1	Jørgensen's Answer to the Dilemma	147

        8.3.1   Jørgensen's Answer to the Dilemma 147

        8.3.2   Ross' Answer to the Dilemma 149

    8.4 Kelsen's Battle against the Dilemma 155

        8.4.1   Correcting Jørgensen 156

        8.4.2   Correcting Ross 158

        8.4.3   Kelsen's Final Solution 160

    8.5 Any Objections? Von Wright's Deontic Logic 162

    8.6 Final Remarks on this Topic 165

9.   The Notion of Practical Reasoning (Part II) 167

    9.1 Dialogs about Kelsen's Solution 168

    9.2 The Dialogical Approach to Logic 170

        9.2.1   Dialog, Validity, Truth and Justification 172

    9.3 The (Dia)logical Tools 176

        9.3.1   Preliminary Notions 176

        9.3.2   Set F Facts and the Problem of Justification 179

        9.3.3   The N Normative System 184

      9.4   The Dialogical System DLLC2...189

      9.5   Jérôme C.'s Guilt and Further Discussions 189

        9.5.1   Jérôme C.'s Example 190

        9.5.2   Further Discussions 193

      9.6   Back to Jørgensen's Dilemma and Final Remarks 196

10. Final Remarks 199

    Appendix 208

    Bibliography..211

Chapter 1

Introduction

The present book represents a true effort in bringing closer two disciplines which have a long history of mutual collaborations but also of remarkable tensions. By the way, the undeniable connections between law and philosophy have already generated a hybrid discipline called "philosophy of law". This special branch aims to studying questions concerning the fundaments of law, the justification of legal norms, the sources of law and also its fundamental notions and concepts such as that of justice, for example, as well as the relations between the legal and the moral field.

But the field of legal philosophy is a very vast one, since it tries to cover different issues conforming the different aspects of the legal domain, such as constitutional law, international law, contract law, and so on. Then, it seems reasonable that an interdisciplinary study must, to begin with, find its specific place and have a specific objective and justification within this legal context. So, for the present study, we have chosen to place our inquiry in the field of legal theory and, more specifically, the field of analytical jurisprudence.

Nowadays, the multidisciplinary feature seems to be a positive quality on the academic context. But the interests in interdisciplinarity are not recent: Logic and Law are a perfect example of two disciplines that were intimate related already when the period of Roman law prevailed. Nevertheless, the results of the possible associations are not always positive ones, and can sometimes be not only mediocre but also disastrous. Gabbay and Woods express the idea of the necessity of a yet prudent perspective, as it follows:

> "For what is interdisciplinary if not a kind of extraterritorial intrusion? It is therefore hardly surprising that most interdisciplinary initiatives fail outright or are dubiously graced by outcomes that are scorned, or merely ignored, by the home disciplines."

It seems that the motto to keep in mind when heading for such an undertaking is the idea that, in the end, the "original" disciplines involved must also somehow profit from the results that may be achieved. We hope it will be the case concerning the present study.

The scope of our investigation concerns the very basic questions involving the normative field, and among them, the most philosophical one might be that of questioning what the exact criterion would be to identify and circumscribe the notion of a legitimate legal norm, i.e. what is that makes us recognize a determined norm coming from law as a binding norm on our behavior. It is in the context of such a problematic that the concepts, notions and theses we will analyze will be inserted.

This perspective allows us to develop the present study according to our general purpose of offering a clear panorama of the possible relations between some legal and philosophical concepts that are often used to deal with the aforementioned questions. This is also the context by excellence of the so-called analytic jurisprudence.

In the context of analytical jurisprudence, the questions about the "nature" of legal norms will be approached by three main schools of thought: the natural law tradition, legal realism and legal positivism. Then, the various philosophers of law will have perspectives more or less explicit in relation to the precepts defended by those three schools. Moreover, the discussion goes so far in time that we can identify such ancient traditions such as Ciceron and the stoics as defenders of the natural law theory perspective, together with the medieval and modern versions defended by Thomas Aquinas, Samuel von Pufendorf and Gottfried Wilhelm Leibniz. Then, more recently, Jeremy Bentham, John Austin, Herbert Hart and, of course, Hans Kelsen can be seen as strict defenders of the legal positivist approach.

Within the frame of legal positivism, which is the legal context we decided to place our investigations, there are numerous concepts and thesis concerning the legal normative field that seem to be very fruitful for a philosophical discussion. On the same way, this approximation with a philosophical perspective also seems to somehow promote confusion and misunderstandings. The present book offers an overview of the main concepts that can cause this kind of confusions, and gives a systematic study of comparison according to the logical perspective on those concepts and the respective legal survey, taking as background the school of thought of legal positivism.

So, the aim of our work is to compare and analyze some of the notions that are "shared" by law and philosophy, with the objective of promote a legitimate approximation of the two fields, rather than artificial ones, like it is sometimes the case, namely when difficult and complex questions such as the possibility of the application of logic to legal norms are simply taken for granted.

Actually, the problem of the applicability will trespass all the chapters of the present study, since our context concerning law will be provided by the legal theory of the Austrian jurist Hans Kelsen (1881 – 1973), the main name of legal positivism, followed by Herbert Hart (1907 – 1992). It is well-know that Kelsen has a very strong interest in philosophy, attested by the innumerable references in his works, mainly the last one, the *General Theory of Norms* (1979), which is also the piece of work we will be focusing on in the present study. Besides, that interest may be the reason why Kelsen is also known as the greatest philosopher among the jurists, and the greatest jurist among the philosophers. But another important detail is the fact that Kelsen's interest is also marked by a methodological precaution: the almost obsessive explanations about the difference between sentences and norms which, for not being neither true nor false, cannot be corresponded or even compared to sentences, falling then "automatically" outside the scope of logical application.

As we will explain further in the following chapters, legal positivism represents a suitable frame for these conceptual analyses due to its methodological soundness, especially under the Kelsenian perspective. By now, let us present the content of the present work as it is divided and organized according to the following chapters:

In chapter 2, we introduce the author and the theory we will be using to frame our approach to the legal domain. As we have already mentioned, we are basing our study in the positivist legal theory proposed by Hans Kelsen, namely in his last book (published posthumously, six years after his passing) called *General Theory of Norms*, of 1979. We will also present the three aforementioned schools of thought in order to justify our preference for the positivist approach, especially concerning the relations between law and philosophy.

In chapter 3, our aim is to provide a general overview of Kelsen's project to Law. That was an essential step to take, since Kelsen introduces several concepts and thesis that are original and fundamental for the approaching of the problems we are dealing with. So, even if the notions introduced in this chapter are going to be taken up again in the next chapters, it seemed useful to present them as a general frame, since most of the concepts play an important role also in the general question of the possibilities of relation between law (norms) and logic.

In chapter 4, we insist on the relevance of legal positivism as an authentic background for the comparison and analysis of the "shared" legal and logic/philosophic notions. This is demonstrated by taking as a counter-example the case of the natural law tradition, which is intrinsically related to subjective or metaphysical notions that fall outside the scientific, objective profile of a legal scientific theory. At the same time, we propose an original approach which could attenuate the methodological tensions between the two antagonist schools of though.

In chapter 5, we take the case of a special kind of fallacy, introduced first by the famous Scottish philosopher David Hume, and later named as the naturalistic fallacy. We investigate the use that Kelsen makes of the notion of naturalistic fallacy in the context of is "pure" theory of law, as a means to prevent the mixing of the legal science with the object it describes, namely, the legal norms. In our view, Kelsen's usage of the fallacy represents an effort towards the approximation between the fields of law and philosophy.

In chapter 6, we analyze the presence of a notion that could be harmful to the thesis of the "purity" of the positive legal theory, namely, the notion of Basic Norm as a fiction. We investigate the correct place of that norm – legal system or legal science? – , an element that, despite not having any prescriptive force or even any content, must still be considered "as-if" it was a "regular" norm in order to perform its function. The philosophical treatment of the notion of fiction as it is used by Kelsen is furnished by the philosophy of "as-if" of the German philosopher Hans Vaihinger.

In chapters 7, 8 and 9, we study the two cases where the application of logic is especially taken under consideration by Kelsen, namely, the problem of the application of the principle of non-contradiction in the case of normative conflicts and the problem of the application of the rule of inference in the case of the creation of a new norm.

In chapter 7, the case of normative conflicts is analyzed based on the function of the derogation norm as a means to legitimately solve the conflict without appealing to logic. We also consider the cases of the losing of normative validity (and, therefore, of existence) due to temporal aspects, as well as the notion of efficacy, since it also plays a major role in the cases when a norm is supposed to (or happens to) lose its validity.

In chapter 8 and 9, the special case of the application of the rule of inference to the situations of normative creation is considered via the notion of practical reasoning. Accepting and defending the legitimacy of practical reasoning and practical syllogism represents to fall in the pit of puzzles and dilemmas such as the Jørgensen's dilemma, which is also treated in those two chapters.

Thus, in chapter 8, we start by explaining the dilemma, as well as two attempts to solve it. Next, we present Kelsen's critics to those treatments of the problem, as well as his own attempt to an answer. His approach will be based on the important notion of modally indifferent substrate as representing the neutral normative content to be inserted either in a normative form or in an indicative one.

Chapter 9 represents a joint work with Dr. Sébastien Magnier, where we aim a treatment of legal creation by means of a different kind of logical approach based of the dialogical approach to logic. This treatment manages to respect and preserve the "purist" character of the positivist legal theory as proposed by Kelsen. This is also our original contribution to the context of problems such as Jørgensen's dilemma.

Lastly, we present the conclusions that can be drawn from the set of conceptual analyses that have been developed in all the previous chapters.

So, to sum up, as we perceive it, Kelsen's approach represents a tireless effort in preserving legal theory as an autonomous field regarding other sciences. Nevertheless, concepts like the naturalistic fallacy and the fictions represent a mode of approximating the fields of philosophy and law, regarding the scientific means (logic, for example) which legal theory may use in order to approach its objects, namely, the legal norms. However, at the same time, we observe Kelsen's worries about taking this relation for granted, especially concerning the particular logical notions of the rule of inference and the principle of non-contradiction as purely logical ones (and never juridical). This kind of "methodological attitude" represents a mistake already pointed out in History of Philosophy by authors like David Hume: it actually constitutes a fallacy, named the naturalistic fallacy. Even so, logic is still nowadays claimed to be an efficient tool used to approach legal norms, instead of being limited to the study of legal theories, a scientific domain where its application is without a doubt legitimate and fruitful.

In front of such a context, the argument that can be sustained is that the philosophical notions which are "welcomed" in the legal field are always supposed to perform in the scientific level, so that they never specifically act over the norms in such a way as to modify the legal system where they are directed to study.

Chapter 2

The Author and his Theory

> *"Hans Kelsen is unquestionably the leading jurist of the time."*
> (Roscoe Pound, 1934)

Perhaps one of the most well-known features of Hans Kelsen's legal theory concerns his attempts towards a "pure" theory of norms. Contrarily to other conceptions and theses[1], the notion of "purity" will be preserved along all of Kelsen's works, more or less explicit conforming the phase. The notion of "purity" as a methodological guideline also represents a special feature of legal positivism when compared to other schools of thought, in the sense that it presupposes rigid boundaries enclosing the legal normative level as, also, the object of legal science.

In this sense, legal positivism establishes that only the "legal" can be source of Law. In the same way, legal norms are going to be defined based only in the legal sources for their creation, by no means appealing to elements outside that legal sphere. In this chapter we will see how this positivistic

---

[1] Kelsen is also known for drastically changing is approach to certain points of his works, creating "phases" in his theory. This includes the problem of the application of Logic as well.

approach contrasts to other schools of thought, namely the Legal Realism and the Natural Law tradition.

The choice for this author as the name we have elected to represent legal Positivism is explained by the very sound philosophical background traversing Kelsen's writings: while the *Pure Theory of Law*[2] is marked by Kelsen's Kantian phase, his later works advanced further from this approach towards a more analytical perspective, were the preoccupations about the influence of Logic in the legal practice have also grown more and more strong with the passing of time, culminating in his posthumous work, the *General Theory of Norms*[3], where the problem of the application of Logic to norms is practically at the core.

2.1 Three Schools of Thought, or: Why Legal Positivism?

It's a well-known fact that Kelsen's most famous work is the *Pure Theory of Law*, whose second edition of 1960 represents the canon of the legal school of thought called Positivism. Legal Positivism represents, together with the Natural Law tradition and the legal Realism, the main currents in legal theory.

The main objective of Hans Kelsen in the *Pure Theory of Law* is to establish a scientifically oriented theory of Law, having the notion of "purity" as a *leitmotif*. Kelsen aims to "purify" the legal method from every possible interference coming from external elements in the description of the legal concepts. Those influences would possibly come from fields such as politics, psychology or sociology, among others. For a positivist, it's easy to notice the

---

[2] Kelsen, H. (1960).
[3] Kelsen, H. (1979).

possible influence of those disciplines in the other schools of thought, which would be, according to Kelsen, a negative aspect attempting against an important feature of the very concept of science: objectivity.

A good way to understand legal Positivism is by noticing how it differs from its "contestant" schools of thought. Each of those schools will try to respond to questions such as what is the right definition of a legal norm (as opposite to other directives such as orders or commandments, or even to other kinds of also binding norms such as those coming from moral systems). They also establish the foundations of a legal system, that is, they try to give an answer to the question of when does an agglomerate of norms could be considered a full normative system.

In the following sections we will present their respective answers to those fundamental questions.

2.1.1 *Legal realism*

Legal realism is the branch of study of legal norms mainly committed to the *efficacy* of the norm as being the main element defining it. A criterion for defining a legal system must then be based in its high effectiveness, meaning that the norms composing the system must be systematically applied and observed in reality[4].

Legal realism is until nowadays represented by the American tradition based on case law and, as it might seem straightforward by the very definition, by

---

[4] The content of the norm must be *observed* by, for example, the citizens, and in the case when this does not happen, then the sanction linked to the lacking of the commanded behavior must be *applied* by the authorities.

the Common Law traditions. Even if those traditions defend a neat autonomy from Morals, Religion (thus averting the Natural Law conceptions) and Politics, the frontiers seem much more blurred when it comes to Sociology, for example. The reason for that is because of the fact that, instead of explaining and justifying how the subjects *should* behave, the theory seem to simply describe how they *actually* behave: the legitimate norm is an efficient one, and the actual behavior serves as model for the prescribed behavior contained in the legal norm. It is easy to notice that aspect especially in the case of common Law, where the norm literally emerges from the custom or from traditional and "standard" practices. A legal system is, by this perspective, simply reduced to a collection of specific cases. If we may already introduce Kelsen's terminology[5], the Realism doesn't step out of the "Is" realm of the descriptions of the facts occurring in the everyday life.[6]

The main name defending the precepts of legal Realism is that of the American jurist Oliver Wendell Holmes Jr. (1841 – 1935), who established the fundaments of this school of thought, being therefore also its founder[7]. Later on, further developments of this theory were attempting to drawn more moderate approaches, but still fundamentally based on and reduced to the American tradition[8].

The critics that can be drawn to this approach are fundamentally based on the fact that legal theory, differently from Sociology, must not explain facts in the same manner as natural science does, i.e. by following the principle of causality that explains how nature "works", but it should rather explain how

---

[5] To be further developed in the following sections of this chapter.
[6] This level is separated from the "Ought" level of the prescriptions, the normative level of Law.
[7] For a general and traditional overview of the theory of legal Realism, see Holmes, O. W. (1881).
[8] The *American Law Institute* might be the most remarkable example among those initiatives.

the legal norms are justified and legitimated. That means: the object of a legal science is not the actual behavior of the agents, but the legal norms themselves. This factor shifts the domain in which we are placing our discourse: a legal science, a legal school of thought, must deal with the legal norms which are, in their nature, prescriptions, imperatives, special kinds of commands. As a legal scientist, one has then to step out of the "Is" level and step into the "Ought" level of normativity to approach their subject of study, since norms act by qualifying those facts: they are not in the same level anymore. The ultimate problem about Realism is that this normative aspect is ignored and norms are dealt as social facts ruled by the principle of causality.

It is clear that Law is also a social phenomenon among others, and can evidently be studied also by Sociology. But the results will not serve to explain the validity of a legal system or, more precisely, its *objective* validity. Legal science must be able to "untie" the objective form out of the multiple particular contents composing different legal systems, in order to rationalize and construct a general objective theory. Departing from this general frame, the jurist will then be able to approach and interpret the many instantiations belonging to different jurisdictions.

2.1.2. *Natural Law Theory*

The Natural Law perspective has a long and solid tradition, drawn either by jurist as well as by (famous) philosophers. The tradition goes back to the *ius naturale* belonging to the Roman law systems. A good impression of what the term *natural law* meant in the context of Roman law can be illustrated by the words of the Roman jurist Gaius (AD 130–180) when he says the following:

> "Every people (*populus*) that is governed by statutes and customs (*leges et mores*) observes partly its own peculiar law and partly the common law of all mankind. That law which a people established for itself is peculiar to it and is called *ius civile* (civil law) as being the special law of that *civitas* (state), while the law that natural reason establishes among all mankind is followed by all peoples alike, and is called *ius gentium* (law of nations, or law of the world) as being the law observed by all mankind. Thus the Roman people observe partly its own peculiar law and partly the common law of all mankind."[9]

It is interesting to notice that the *ius gentium*, in this context, was considered as a mere part or an aspect of the broader *ius naturale*. Slightly different approaches of the notion of natural law can also be found, among others, in the Stoic philosophical tradition[10], namely in the words of Cicero, when he says the famous words:

> "True law is right reason in agreement with nature; it is of universal application, unchanging and everlasting; it summons to duty by its commands, and averts from wrongdoing by its prohibitions... It is a sin to try to alter this law, nor is it allowable to repeal any part of it, and it is

---

[9] Gaius cited by Winkel, L. (2004, p. 225).
[10] And also during modern philosophy. This issue will be further developed in Chapter 4.

impossible to abolish entirely. We cannot be freed from its obligations by senate or people, and we need not look outside ourselves for an expounder or interpreter of it."[11]

During the medieval period, the natural law tradition suffered from a strong influence of Christianity, especially regarding the works of Thomas Aquinas (1225 – 1274). There is a shifting of the source of Law, which no longer is established by Reason and marked by some kind of "rational self-evidence" as in the Antiquity, but established by God and marked by the "universal" values of *good* and *just*. Let us consider the following passage from Thomas Aquinas:

> "(...) there belongs to the natural law, first, certain most general precepts, that are known to all; and secondly, certain secondary and more detailed precepts, which are, as it were, conclusions following closely from first principles. As to those general principles, the natural law, in the abstract, can nowise be blotted out from men's hearts. But it is blotted out in the case of a particular action, insofar as reason is hindered from applying the general principle to a particular point of practice, on account of concupiscence or some other passion, as stated above. But as to the other, i.e., the secondary precepts, the natural law can be blotted out from the human heart, either by evil persuasions, just as in speculative matters errors occur in respect of necessary conclusions; or by vicious customs and corrupt habits, as

---

[11] Cicero cited by Wood, N. (1988, p. 71).

among some men, theft, and even unnatural vices, as the Apostle states (Rm. i), were not esteemed sinful."[12]

Later, Samuel Pufendorf (1632 – 1694), John Locke (1632 – 1704) and Gottfried Wilhelm Leibniz (1646 – 1716) might all be cited as good examples of a naturalist legal perspective based on theological foundations.

So, while legal realism is limited to the description of Law *qua* social phenomenon, natural law engages with the evaluation and qualification of the reality. The criterion to legitimate and define a norm is no longer based in its factual efficacy, but rather in a judgment of value, such as the *good* or the *just*.

It is then easy to notice the methodological problems of such an approach in the context of the construction of a legal theory: the natural law theory is based on a subjective criterion for the definition of Law. It gets involved with ideologies and becomes doctrine rather than science. It is important to remark that we are not defending the legal norms don't have to be just (neither is the legal positivism or the legal realism): the point is that justice cannot be the measurement to define a norm, given that this definition has to be based in an objective criterion.

2.1.3 *Legal Positivism*

---

[12] Aquinas, T. (2014[1265–1274] I-II qq. 90-106).

Perhaps the very first remark to be made about the current of legal positivism should be that it sees Law as a human construction, as something that didn't exist before human's will. This first aspect will give then space to all further differences when comparing it with the previous schools we have just presented.

The criteria for a norm to be defined as a legally binding one is, according to legal positivism, its very own existence as a norm, that is, that fact of being "correctly" enacted or "posited". The specific existence of a norm it's called *legal validity*. Only "posited" norms are valid, or are consider as existent within the frame of a determined legal order. In order to be valid, a norm must also be enacted by an authorized person, whose competence is attributed by the Law itself. In the case of the Kelsenian theory, we might recognize the fact that this is indeed the closest one can get to the notion of "purity".

Natural lawyers will then attack the legal positivism by turning the attention to the troublesome fact that, whatever content the norm will have, if it is still enacted and posited according to the form predicted by the positivists, it will be a legitimate, valid, binding norm. In this sense, the form "despises" the content. The function of the jurist will be, then, to simply limit himself to impartially interpret this norm without questioning its value: if it's good, moral, just…

This problem continues to be evoked nowadays, and constitutes nothing more than a miscomprehension of the finality of a legal theory. The problem of unjust or "bad" laws is a legitimate one and should be dealt with most tenacity. But the point is that it is not the function of the legal science to do so. The verification of the validity of a norm has nothing to do with the subjective evaluation of its content and its practical consequences. That difference is based on the classical fact-value distinction, constant in every serious scientific context. Norberto Bobbio explains very well – as he always does – this problematic confusion when he writes:

> "In the same way, the fact that racial laws (to repeat the same example that the modern moralists from law resort to) are iniquitous didn't prevent that they, unfortunately, existed, and that they have not only been valid, but also efficient regarding the way they have been applied and have found enthusiastic executors, along with an inert mass of accomplices. And if they have existed, it's clear that the problem of their validity, application or interpretation was, in the orders they belonged to, a different problem than that of their evaluation."[13]

Nevertheless, one could still argue that the critics coming from the natural law theorists are not about the laws already enacted in the past, but rather that the legal positivism should not allow those laws to become valid or legitimate, so that the laws concerning slavery, for example, should never have existed in the first place. In this case we should again remember that the function of the jurist is not that of dictating or influencing the creation or the content of norms, but rather to study and interpret those laws in an impartial manner. Admitting the contrary is to give to the science an apologetic aspect that simply cannot be seriously considered.

---

[13] Bobbio, N. (2008, p.26). This passage is a personal translation from the version in Portuguese.

2.2 **Why Kelsen?**

It becomes now clearer why the legal theory of Hans Kelsen represents a good frame of study of the relations between Law and Philosophy. More precisely, the philosophical aspects that seemed to interest Kelsen are those belonging specially to the field of Logic. Kelsen's aim is to develop a theory for the knowledge of the legal material, to provide a criterion for giving to the conjunction of multiple norms an objective rational unity.

The full commitment with the notion of "purity" regarding his approach to legal science will later reveal itself to be a sober position about the common practice of application of logic to the object of that science, namely, the legal norms.

2.2.1. *The historical context*

Hans Kelsen was born in Prague, in 1881. His family moved to Vienna in 1884, where Kelsen studied Law at the University of Vienna. His doctorate thesis concerned the reading of Dante's Divine Comedy as a complex political metaphor. This approximation with Dante Alighieri's work, strongly marked by a catholic perspective, made the young Kelsen – originally coming from a Jewish family – convert to Roman Catholicism in 1905[14].

In 1911, Kelsen accomplished his *Habilitation* in Public Law and Legal Philosophy, which is the academic qualification allowing to hold lectures and

---

[14] Seven years later Kelsen will get married and convert to Lutheranism.

to supervise doctoral candidates. Right after this achievement, Kelsen was able to work as a full professor at the University of Vienna. It was during this period that he worked on the draft of the Austrian Constitution, enacted in 1920. Kelsen's version is by the way the one still nowadays in effect.

During the 1930ies, Kelsen had grown more active in the political discussions of his time, especially regarding the totalitarian profile of rising government. This was also the year when Kelsen moved to Germany, working as a professor in the University of Cologne.

Three years later, the National Socialism rose in Germany and Kelsen immediately moved to Geneva, in Switzerland. During this period, Kelsen also supervised the *Habilitation* thesis of Hans Morgenthau (1904 – 1980). The two worked together in actively condemning and criticizing the German National Socialism, due to what both became *persona non grata* in the German territory during the entire prevalence of this regime. Morgenthau became a lifetime friend of Kelsen, and later would become a famous name in the field of international politics, working also as a consultant for the Kennedy administration in the United States from 1961 to 1963.

In the year of 1934, Kelsen publishes the first edition of the *Pure Theory of Law*. He continues working in Vienna until 1940, when he decides to move to the United States to work at the Harvard Law School. In 1945 he becomes full professor at the University of California, Berkeley, where we would work for the rest of his life. There, he would later publish the second edition of the *Pure Theory of Law*, in 1960, at the age of 78, achieving the work that represents undoubtedly a major breakthrough in the field of legal theory.

In was during his mature years, especially after the 1960ies, that Kelsen's interest in the matters concerning the possibility of a logic of legal and moral norms started to grow. By the year of his death, in 1973, Kelsen had collected a vast quantity of notes on this subject, which were organized and published posthumously, in 1979, under the title of *General Theory of Norms*.

Because of its special focus on the relations between logic and Law, and the very "philosophically oriented" regard that Kelsen offers to his positivist approach to legal theory, the *General Theory of Norms* is the main reference we will be using for the present study. Nevertheless, the main notions and methodological precepts were, in their great majority, already introduced in the second edition of the *Pure Theory of Law*. Let us see more carefully how they were approached in those two main kelsenian works.

2.2.2. *The Pure Theory of Law (1960)*

The second edition of the *Pure Theory of Law* came to be the most known work of Kelsen, and is where he introduces and explains many of the notions that will traverse the rest of his writings. Nevertheless, some of the theses presented in the book were drastically modified and corrected in the following works. This applies to the matter of the application of the logic to norms (where Kelsen still admits, in this book, an "indirect" application by analogy, to be later on, in the 1979's publication, transformed into a full refutation) and also concerning the notion of Basic Norm (that here is still seen as a hypothesis, to be later on regarded as a fiction), for example.

But it's in the *Pure Theory of Law* that Kelsen entirely commits himself to the methodological profile that will mark his entire work. The notion of "purity", the methodological abyss between "Is" and "Ought", the notion of legal validity as existence, the refutation of the notion of practical reasoning, the hierarchical disposition of the norms in the legal system according to a "pyramidal" figure, will all shape the further developments to be present in the later *General Theory of Norms*[15], the last work of his, where Kelsen philosophically profoundly analyses his concepts and thesis while comparing them to traditional philosophic and legal theories and vigorously responding to critics.

The *Pure Theory of Law* is also the piece of work that marks a Kantian phase of Kelsen's conceptions. Kelsen himself confirms this when he writes, in a letter of 1933 to Renato Treves, that: "*It is altogether correct that the philosophical foundation of the* Pure Theory of Law *is the Kantian philosophy*"[16]. With this perspective, Kelsen was actually trying to apply the transcendental method to his theory. In the *Pure Theory of Law*, Kelsen tries to investigate at a great length the following problem:

> "Kant asks: 'How, without appealing to metaphysics, can the facts perceived by our senses be interpreted in the laws of nature, as these are formulated by natural science?'. In the same way, the Pure Theory of Law asks: "How, without appealing to meta-legal authorities like God or nature, can the subjective sense of certain material facts be interpreted as a system of objectively valid legal norms that are describable in legal propositions?"[17]

The answer given by Kelsen will be based on the notion of Basic Norm in its hypothetical expression, a presupposition to be assumed by the legal scientist in his cognitive reference to the norms of a determined legal system.

---

[15] Kelsen (1979).
[16] Kelsen (1998 [1933], p.171).
[17] Kelsen (1960, p. 202).

Thus, if in the *Pure Theory of Law* the philosophical questions are oriented towards epistemic and methodological matters; in the subsequent *General Theory of Norms* it is the possibility of logical relations between those legal norms that is the problem which seems to affect Kelsen the most.

2.2.3 *The General Theory of Norms (1979)*

One could easily defend that the discussion around the topic of the possibility of a logic of norms might be the main subject of the *General Theory of Norms*. If there are nevertheless other important issues discussed in the book, as for example the different linguistic expressions concerning the norms, their functions and their relation to science, all those matters seem to lead to this main discussion, trying to give the arguments for the denial of the possibility to apply traditional bivalent logic to legal norms.

Also, as the title suggests, Kelsen proposes a theory not only for legal norms, but also for those of positive morals. Nevertheless, it does not seem that their identification is actually straightforward. Even if Kelsen mostly illustrates his conceptions with examples coming from the moral domain (especially from positive religious morality, such as Christianity), some legal features are more difficult to be recognized in the moral field. One example might be the case of normative conflicts which, in the moral domain, seem to be more similar to moral dilemmas, which are treated completely differently from normative conflicts. The notion of derogation sounds also very artificial when applied in the moral level. Moreover, another remarkable difference concerns the notion of delict and sanctions: even if the morality also "punishes" the behavior to be avoided, that conception of sanction is much looser, and less "institutionalized", let us say, when compared to the legal one. Outside the religious level, the notion of "authorization" also becomes problematic, which is clearly noticed when we attempt to the fact that Kelsen always appeals to limited examples displaying paternal relations, such as a father giving an order to his son, or of a teacher in relation to the student.

Back to the main question of the applicability of logic to norms, two paths are used in Kelsen's argumentation concerning this problem: the denial of application of the rule of inference in the case of normative creation, and the denial of the application of the principle of non-contradiction in the case of normative conflicts. The *motto* of the whole discussion lies on the fact that norms, since neither true or false, are not able to be logically treated in the same way as sentences are.

Kelsen offers this extreme negative position concerning the applicability as an answer to the common practice of using law to deal with norms: *"That they (the principle of non-contradiction and the rules of inference) are applicable to norms of positive law has been almost universally assumed in traditional legal theory"*.[18]

Due to this critical perspective, this book offers us a perfect frame for our study. In our view, the general hesitation on understanding and accepting Kelsen's theory as well as his strong position regarding the logical applicability is aggravated for two main reasons:

1) From the part of the juridical community: the discussions about the possible relations between law and philosophy (mainly logic) are obscured because of the extent to which Kelsen carried on his formalist project: Kelsen

---

[18] Kelsen, H.(1979, p. 189).

is interested in building a rigorous scientific general theory, and his discourse might sound "empty" to the jurist who is interest in solving the problems he/she faces in the everyday practice of law. Even if those problems have to do with legal theory, it's not in the work of Kelsen that the answers will be found. For example: an important actual problem in Law can be found in the context of normative conflicts. The jurist, or the lawyer, are interested in knowing, in the context of a situation of two different norms being capable of rule one specific case, which of them should be picked up. The hidden element behind the possible choice is the intention of the legislator or of the higher authority while enacting the norm. It would be very useful to have then some kind of principle ruling this kind of conflict or dilemma, in the same way that logic has its own principle of non-contradiction. But Kelsen's theory will nor answer to this kinds of "practical" questions: it will rather give us a formal frame of the situation of conflict in law, while insisting on the fact that a normative conflict should not be treated as a propositional contradiction, because two conflicting norms have to be both valid in order to be in the situation of conflict in the first place, which is very different from the case of contradictions between propositions, which have the property of being true and false at the same time ($A \land \neg A$). So, against the jurist/lawyer expectations, not only the kelsenian theory will not give a practically applicable answer, but will also insist on the fact that the possible answer given by logic is not applicable nor legitimate in the legal field.

2) From the part of the philosophical community: the relations between law and philosophy (mainly logic) are misinterpreted because of the fact that the legal concepts, once apparently similar to the philosophical ones (validity, science, condition, fiction and many others) are frequently confounded with their philosophical counterparts. That means that the concepts receive their usual philosophical approach instead of being regarded within their legal

background (since legal validity is not the same as logical validity, science is not the same as normative science, a legal condition is not the same as a logical condition or conditional and so on).

In the frame of Kelsen's *General Theory of Norms*, those difficulties are put into light. The consequence is that, nowadays, this work of Kelsen is probably the least studied or commented or referred to, despite its great philosophical richness. Kelsen developed, in this piece of work, a thorough discussion between logic and law in order to set and fix the limits on their legitimate approximation. Because of that, the relations are more limited, but also more reliable and more sound.

For the jurist, the text and the problems that are treated seem to remain "too abstract". For the philosophers, only a few would agree that the "practical syllogism", for example, a structure where a norm is derived from another norm together with its factual instantiation, fails as a model to express the "creation" of new specific norms from general norms: they seem to take it for granted, and see as almost natural the relation (and the identification) of a valid norm and a true proposition, probably because of the logical "equivalent" notion of logical validity as meaning "true in all possible worlds", or maybe because of the illusionistic evidence showed by the multiple everyday examples such as those displaying at Jørgensen's dilemma…

We propose, in the following chapters, a detailed study of the relations between those apparently "shared" notions. The results might better explain why it is still so hard to put into practice what is attested in the theory.

Our aim is not to establish a complete separation between the fields of law and philosophy (and logic), but rather to establish a legitimate dialog, by respecting the autonomy of the two domains and the impassable particularities that make them two specific areas of their own.

Chapter 3

Preliminary Notions

"A theory that explains everything, explains nothing"
Karl Popper

In order to develop the analysis and comparisons between Law and Philosophy in the manner intended in the present work, we must first of all introduce the principal notions and arguments proposed by the legal Positivism as it is seen by the legal theorist Hans Kelsen. The criteria for the choosing of the concepts approached in this chapter are based on their "similarity" or "approximation" to important concepts belonging to the philosophical field. This represents somehow a problem, in the sense that, in the attempts of building connections between the legal and philosophical field, those notions can be confounded and then interpreted and applied in a wrong manner. Our attempt is precisely to clarify how far we can go in those attempts, by elucidating and preserving the notions' particularities. Besides, this work might even – we hope so – reinforce the dialog between the two disciplines, since it preserves a legitimate and thus reliable relation between them.

Moreover, the important aspect to be taken into account in this context is the problem of the possibility of application of logic to norms. Most of the legal notions we will face have some kind of "counterpart" in the logic tradition. This means that the notions share the same name, but not the same meaning. The most remarkable is the case of the notion of validity. Legal validity, in the tradition of legal positivism, has a drastically different meaning that the validity studied by logic. This represents a major problem in the context of the matter of the logical treatment of those norms, where this notion of validity is mostly misinterpreted.

However, before approaching those problems in the different chapters of the present study, let us first introduce a general overview of the main concepts that will be involved in the philosophical reading of legal positivism.

We will dedicate special sections in this chapter to, respectively, the notions of legal validity as related to that of logical validity; the methodological separation between "Is" and "Ought" and the naturalistic fallacy; the presence of fictions in law, specially the case of the Basic norm in the legal positivism and the question of non-existence; legal conditions as opposed to logical conditionals; the notion o temporality in Law in the context of conflicting norms and their relation to contradictory propositions and, last but not least, Kelsen's denial of the practical syllogism (and the application of the rule of inference)as a means to express the normative creation.

Those topics are therefore explained by taking as a background – more or less explicitly depending on the subject in question – the problem of the possibility of application of logic to norms.

3.1. The notion of legal validity

The first step when approaching the notion of legal validity in the positivist context is to understand its identification with the *specific existence* of a norm. So, if validity is identified with the mode of existence of a norm, let us see how the positivist tradition arrives at this definition.

3.1.1 *Defining "legal norm"*

At first glance, it is easy to understand norms as being the meaning of something that happens in reality and, after a specific interpretation, constitutes a norm. Let us consider the following case, for example: if I want something to happen or someone to behave in a certain matter, I express this will with an act, which Kelsen calls an *act of will* or an *act of commanding*. It is simply the expression of one's "wanting" something to happen. It can be a linguistic act, a sign drew on a board or a plank, a rising of a hand, a whistle... Then, this act has to be interpreted in a specific manner – receive a legal meaning – in order to be understood as a norm. In this sense, the linguistic act will be interpreted as an order from a Judge, for example; the sign in the board will be interpreted as a limitation of speed in traffic, the rising of a hand will be interpreted as a voting in a parliament, and the whistle will be interpreted as a permission to cross the street. The norms which represent these meanings should not be identified with the acts themselves, which are something factual occurring in reality and ruled by the principle of causality. They merely "create" the norm, in the sense of positing it. It is easy to understand how they are independent and should be separated from each other in this aspect when we consider that the norm created by the act must continue to rule even when the act or the willing of its author ceases to exist[19].

Also, one important detail is that those acts will only be directly related to Law if they can receive a legal interpretation. Otherwise they might be norms (in a weaker sense) but not binding legal norms. The means to establish the possibility of this legal interpretation is given by a more general norm, present in the legal order, which rules the situation where the "new" norm emerges. Then, considering the abovementioned linguistic act of the Judge, for example, the act is capable of receiving a legal interpretation because there is a "higher" already existing legal norm that gives to the Judge the capacity, the authorization, to emit such an act of will.

Departing from this scenario, we can now introduce the very basic positivist definition of a legal norm as a specific meaning:

> "The norm is the meaning of a willing or act of will and – if the norm is a prescription or a command – it is the meaning of an act directed to the behavior of another person, an act whose meaning is that another person (or persons) is to behave in a certain way".[20]

Moreover, in order to be classified as legal and binding, the meaning of the act of will in question might not be simply subjective (which would then consist in a mere desire or whish towards someone's behavior), but it has to be objective. Objective, in this sense, means that the addressees might recognize it as binding, and not only the person enacting the norm. The

---

[19] Or, more "dramatically" speaking: even after its author's death.
[20] Kelsen, H. (1979, p.2).

element providing that objectiveness is the notion of empowering, or authorization. The person enacting the act of will must be authorized (by Law) in order to produce binding norms as the meaning of his act of will. At this point we can introduce this important precision made by Kelsen:

> "This is the only way in which the command of a highwayman can be distinguished from that of a moral or legal authority. Generally: not every Ought which is the meaning of an act of will is a binding norm. For instance: I can will 'Everyone is to marry upon reaching a certain age'. That is not a binding norm for there is no norm of a positive moral or legal order which empowers me to posit such a norm. The Ought in this case is only the subjective meaning of my act of will, and not its objective meaning. It is only when the Ought has an objective meaning, and so expresses a command, that there exists a duty (i.e. a binding norm)."[21]

According to Kelsen, the statements are, by their turn, the meaning of acts of thought, described in propositions which can be then evaluated as true of false. But this is no longer the normative domain of the "Ought", ruled by the principle of imputation, but merely the indicative domain of the "Is", ruled by causality.

The notion of *objectiveness* is also essentially linked to that of *validity*, since only when the norm is the objective meaning of act of will it is also said to be a valid norm, i.e., to exist within the frame of a determined legal order.

---

[21] Kelsen, H. (1979, p. 27).

3.1.2 *Validity as Existence*

We have seen that the theory of legal positivism, contrarily to the natural law and the legal realism traditions, aims to preserve the scientific objectiveness by using the notion of legal validity as a criterion for defining a norm and a normative system. This notion is then identified with the objective existence of a norm.

It is a curious fact that "validity" is a common term in Logic and in Law, because the notion hides in reality two drastic different meanings. In Logic, we say from an argument that it is valid due to the logical necessity of the conclusion, given the two premises. Also, a sentence can be said to be valid, if it is true in all possible interpretations. In any case, what is interesting is the fact that the notion of validity in Logic seems to be – in one way or another – somehow linked to the notion of truth.

Now, let's move back to the legal field. For a positivist theorist, the simple definition saying that "When we say 'A norm is valid' we mean that a norm exists", even if it seems almost trivial, it is at the same time a fruitful ground for legal, logical and, mostly, philosophical analysis. Let us see how it happens.

"Philosophically speaking", we have to understand that, even if norms have a linguistic formulation, even if they somehow give information, if they are written in the Constitution or fixed in the walls of the public swimming pools of our cities, they are not to be treated as normal sentences. What the positivist claim is saying is that norms have existence! In this sense, when the legal norms exist, they are also, at the same time, "automatically" said to be valid. Their existence is their validity.

This claim is fully committed with the idea of *positing* a norm which is, clearly enough, essential to the legal positivism. Kelsen declares that *"From the point of view of ethical and legal positivism, the only norms considered to be objects of cognition are positive norms, that is, norms posited by acts of will, and indeed, by human acts of will."*[22] Kelsen distinguishes the norms which are the meaning of those "real" acts of will from the norms which are the meaning of a fictitious act of will – such as the Basic Norm. Fictitious acts of will won't generate norms with specific existence, but only with a fictional one. They do not really exist in the frame of a determined legal order, and that is the sense in which the term *existence* must be taking in this context.

Thus, validity is the ideal existence of a norm within the context of a determined legal order. Therefore, considering for example the case of the Brazilian norm called the "Pelé" Law (Law N. 9.615/98) enforcing that, by the year of 2001, (soccer) clubs can only sign a maximum five-year contract with a player, and allowing (soccer) clubs to create and promote their own leagues;we must understand that this norm*exists* within the frame of the *"Código Brasileiro de Justiça Desportiva"*, and it *does not exist* in the German Civil Code or the Brazilian Penal Code.

There is still another factor that seems to increase the difficulty for the philosophical understanding of legal norms: the validity is not even a property of a norm, in the same way that we say from a proposition that it has the property of being true or false. Hans Kelsen defines legal validity as the following: *"Validity is the specific existence of a norm, an existence different from that of a natural fact, and in particular from that of the fact by*

---

[22] Kelsen, H. (1979, p.4).

which it is created. A norm decrees an Ought"[23]. And if the norm decrees an ought, it has a normative function, that of commanding, empowering, permitting or derogating. To say that a norm is valid is in fact a pleonasm, when norms are invalid, they are not binding, they are not part of the legal set that constitutes Law, they are anywhere![24] Invalid norms are in fact simply commands, orders, norms-to-be, without legal status.

This thesis also finds an echo in the philosophical tradition, namely, in the famous statement of Kant when he says that existence is not a real (as opposed to a logical or syntactical) predicate[25]. In this sense, if existence is not a real predicate or a property; existence is not a characteristic which can be *added* to the concept of the subject. This argument was brought up by Kant concerning the context of the ontological proofs for the existence of God. Kant says:

> "Both (the object and the concept) must contain exactly the same, and hence when I think of this object as given absolutely (through the expression 'it is'), nothing is thereby added to the concept, which expresses merely its possibility. Thus the actual contains nothing more than the merely possible. A hundred actual dollars do not contain the least bit more than the hundred possible ones. For since the latter signifies the concept and the former its object and its positing in itself, then, in case the former contained more

---

[23] Kelsen, H. (1979, P.2).
[24] There's no authorized act of "positing" the norm anywhere.
[25] Which, on its turn, finds an echo in Hume's thesis concerning existence. After Kant, there is also the Frege-Russell view that existence is not a property of individuals.

than the latter, my concept would not express the entire object and thus would not be the suitable concept of it."[26]

We can draw a bridge between the Kelsenian and Kantian perspectives in the sense that both seem to be saying that the existence doesn't "collaborate" in the explanation of a concept. Taking the case of legal norms, it is completely redundant to say that a positive norm exists; in the same way it is redundant to say that a positive norm is valid. The existence and the validity are the very "nature" of the legal norm itself: it is only *as* existing and *as* valid that we can grasp the notion of a positive legal norm.

Differently, "real" predicates such as *good* or *just* or *efficient* actually do add something else to this existent norm, they are properties that tell us something about the norm. We are in this case dealing with two different concepts which are put in relation to each other (for example, that of *justice* and that of *norm*), qualifying and thus broadening the meaning in question.

3.2. Legal Science and its Object: Hume's Naturalistic Fallacy

Now that we have seen what legal positivism follows as a methodological guideline, namely, the notion of "purity", we can analyze how that science approaches its object: the legal norms. The case of legal science is a rather particular one, and very different from natural science. Legal science

---

[26] Kant, I. (1781/1998, 567 [B627=A599]).

describes norms, that is, it makes descriptions about prescriptions. Let us see how that relation is articulated.

A norm can make part of a sentence which can be evaluated as true or false. Sentences about norms, describing norms, are the content of a special kind of science, called normative science or science of Law. Since the normative science contains true/false sentences *about Law* – which is the overall set of norms, which can only be said to be valid – the limits between these two spheres can be often erased, giving place to a number of confusions.

3.2.1 *Hume's Naturalistic Fallacy*

Facts of nature, causal links, scientific discoveries, they are all expressed by sentences, and through our mental/rational evaluation they can be said to be true or false. All of these elements belong to the realm of the "Is". But positive norms are not given facts to be attested, they need to be created, and they are created by intentional acts of human will. When a norm is created as the objective meaning of an act of will, it is said to be valid, and decrees an "Ought". This specificity places the norms in another, particular realm, the normative realm of the "Ought", which is completely separated and not reducible to the indicative realm of the "Is".

This rigid separation is another constant methodological principle guiding the whole positivistic theory. It represents a methodological "abyss" between the realms of the normative – the "Ought" field – and that of the indicative – the "Is" field.

The mistake consisting in mixing those two separated domains represents an error that was already pointed in History of philosophy, called the Naturalistic Fallacy. Even if the term was introduced by G. E. Moore in his *Principia Ethica* of 1903, it is fully inspired on the traditional problem of the is-ought separation approached by the Scottish philosopher David Hume (1711 – 1776) in his *A Treatise of Human Nature* of 1738. While the moorean version was more focused on the problem of identifying *good* with the *object* qualified as good, the humean version is more concerned with the confusion between the domain of the "Is" and that of the "Ought" and the vanishing of the borders separating them.

The context of Hume's criticism is the attempts to "naturalize" morals. In the legal context, those attempts also exists, given that the problem of the fallacy arises precisely together with the efforts to, for example, apply Logic to norms, that is, to treat norms as if there were natural facts described by propositions. In Morals, the fallacy would be to consider "moral properties" as "natural properties", and Ethics as if it were a part of natural sciences. But in Law, the fallacy would mainly be recognized in the efforts to treat legal norms as true/false sentences, instead of the fruit of human arbitrary will.

The necessity and importance concerning a clear borderline between the two fields – factual and normative – is explained by Hume himself: "*Morals excite passions, and produce or prevent actions. Reason itself is utterly impotent in this particular. The rules of morality, therefore, are not conclusions of our reason*"[27].

This also clearly represents a refutation of the notion of practical reasoning, that is, of the possibility of "creating" norms from reason or rational deduction. It is very important to systematically reinforce the idea that,

---

[27] Hume, D. (1739/1985, p. 509).

indeed, norms can also be the meaning of acts of thought, which will give them their content, the information they'll be giving to their addressees (what to do or not to do, and the consequences following...). But that's not yet the moment when the norm is actually posited: this content must be seen as the "material" for the subsequent act of intentionally willing it towards another one's behavior.

Thus, the act of thought is simply a "first step" in the process of normative creation, an can even be ignored, when we take in consideration the case, for example, of a parliament member who votes for the approval of a norm without even knowing its content, i.e., what the norm prescribes. The point is that the meaning of that *action* of the parliament member was the creation of a norm, and it can have nothing to do with the enaction of a description about someone else's behavior, or an evaluation about it or any other mental or rational outcomes.

The naturalistic fallacy is such a common argumentative mistake, that it is easy to recognize it even in everyday examples, as well as in many other levels. Let us then see how the problem of the naturalistic fallacy is identified by another authors, this time with a very contemporary example:

> "So, for example, Peter Singer takes E. O. Wilson to task for committing the mistake of moving 'from is to ought' – specifically, for moving from the premise 'Our genes came from a common pool and will return to a common pool' to the conclusion that 'we ought not to do anything which imperils the human gene pool' (Singer, 1981, p. 80). Singer correctly points out that this argument is invalid as it stands – Wilson has neither made explicit, nor defended as a moral value, the premise: 'We ought not to do anything which

> imperils the long-term survival of our genes'. Then, invoking nothing more than Hume's 'unbridgeable gulf between facts and values', Singer asserts that 'ethical premises are not the kind of thing discovered by scientific investigation' and hence '[n]o science is ever going to discover ethical premises inherent in our biological nature'."[28]

Once the necessity of clear and rigid divisions between "Is" and "Ought" is understood, we can now also understand how the legal science approaches its object of study: the positive legal norms.

3.2.2 *The relations between the Science and its Object*

Concerning precisely the relations between the science and its scientific object – here, legal science and Law itself, it is important to insist on the fact that, even if the legal science deals with valid norms, it doesn't have any normative legal power.

The function of the legal scientist, or the jurist, is that of impartially describe, explain and justify the concepts, theses and procedures followed regarding a determined legal normative system. Within the context of a science, the jurists, while mentioning and repeating the norms in their sentences about their validity, are ascertaining a fact to be verified by simply observing the legal documents. This can only be the case in this context of legal positivism,

---

[28] Curry, O. (2006, p. 238).

where the source of law is directly linked to the "belonging" of the norm to a determined normative system.

Now, since the validity of the norms is also directly linked to the authority of the subject enacting it, positing it, we can clearly remark that the jurist, while producing the theory, has no authority to impregnate the scientific results with prescriptive power, with legal validity or bindingness. The prescriptions of law will, in the context of science, have their validity expressed by sentences, which will be true of false, depending on their correctness, which can be attested by empiric verification.

One fine interpretation is the one that Norberto Bobbio makes of this unusual fact that the normative science makes descriptions about prescriptions. Bobbio didactically explain how the jurist is supposed to "perform" in his task of neutrally describing the norms of a given legal order as the following:

> "One can identify an oscillation and a superposition of two meanings, related but not clearly separated:
> a) the norms, a determined system of norms, are the point of view from which the jurist, differently from the sociologist, considers the social behaviors; they appear through a screen with a certain narrative structure, and the behaviors are of interest once regulated and for the way they are regulated.
> b) normative propositions are the result achieved by the jurist with his work of verification, interpretation and systematization of a determined positive legal order. Maybe we could say the same as the following: being the normative science descriptive, it describes facts qualified as norms, i.e., by norms, or it rather formulates ought-propositions by

> means of assertions. It does not mean that those two meanings for "normative" are not conjugated in the saying expressed many times by Kelsen, that the legal science is normative while it describes what it is, but that in order to describe what ought to be, it makes use of a determined legal system."[29]

The "political" aspect behind that discussion is clearly the matter whether the legal science is normative, i.e., whether it has the function of proposing "better versions" of the norms, or still, whether it should correct norms or somehow "ameliorate" their formulation. Regarding that question, Bobbio introduces the differences between "normative" and "prescriptive" to explain that the normative science, despite the fact of dealing with norms – where the "normative" term comes from –, does not make use of a prescriptive discourse, that is, their descriptions don't have the aim of changing the behavior of others, because they are nevertheless still situated in the domain of the "Is".

Of course that, in the everyday practice, things may not be so black in white. The myth of the "impartial" researcher should, especially in the legal filed, not be entirely believed nor taken for granted. The jurist has a critical reading when describing and interpreting the Law, and perhaps this is even a positive aspect of his/her work. But what we should always keep in mind is the purpose of Kelsen while interested in this kind of science, in providing a general formal theory: he is setting the way the jurist must precede, not the way he/she eventually ends up proceeding.

---

[29] Bobbio, N. (2008, P. 59). This passage is a personal translation from the version in Portuguese.

3.3 Legal Conditions

Now that we have already explained how the definition of the legal norm is identified with a meaning, namely the objective meaning of an act of will, it's time to analyze how the norm is linguistically formulated or constructed.

3.3.1 *Imperatives and Norms*

In order to introduce the discussion about the formulation of a legal norm, we can start by approaching a strictly philosophical concept, namely, Immanuel Kant's notion of "imperative of skill".

Since, to Kant, all imperatives express an ought, the imperative of skill will represents a "norm" in the sense of a "rule" in order to reach an end via determined means. Kant says that: *"All sciences have some practical part which consists of problems of some end which is possible for us and of imperatives as to how it can be reached. These can therefore generally be called imperatives of skill."*[30]

So, according to Kant, an imperative of skill will be expressed in the following imperative form, for instance:

> "If you want water to boil, you ought to heat it to 100°C."

---

[30] Kant, I. (1785/2005, p.56)

But the point is that this means-end relation is clearly a causal relation. And causal relations express a *must*, and not an *ought*, which is the normative component by excellence. The means-end relation expressed by the imperative of skill is not a normative relation; it is not expressed by a norm in the strict sense of the term, and does not posit an obligatory behavior, it rather gives a recommendation, an advice concerning the reaching of a determined objective.

These specifications concerning the Kantian notion of imperative are particularly useful to notice that a norm is not as general as the notion of imperative or command. Indeed, the definition of "norm" is somehow relied to the concept of a command or an order, but with the important detail that this order must come from an authorized person, as an expression – mostly in the form of an imperative – of a will.

Also, since this willing must come from a person authorized by the Law itself, there is always a strict relation between the legal production and the legal power. A subjective act of will consists only in a command, without legal force, it means the expression of a personal willing towards a specific case, and that's not what Law is about. Differently, an objective command is not only the psychic event of the expression of a will. This can be seen in the case of a testament, for instance. In a valid testament, the subjective act of will of the person making the testament obtains its objectivity through the Law: once it is legally legitimated by an authorized person or organ, the command of the person in question will remain valid beyond his own existence, when he will no longer be able to express his subjective will. This demonstrates the independency of the compulsoriness of the command from the subjective act of will.

Kelsen illustrates this point by giving the example of a gangster's demanding for money. When the gangster asks you to give him all your money, this order, or the imperative he emits, has not the same meaning as when the tax officer asks you for the money, namely, that the person towards whom the order is formulated ought to render a determined amount of money. The tax officer's "request" is actually a biding valid legal norm, because it is based on the Law, and the officer has the authority and the power given by the Law itself allowing him to perform in the specific way he does. On the contrary, the gangster's order represents only a subjective act of will (even if it can be really appealing to call it binding, depending on the means he uses to attain the ends), and it has the meaning of a command, but not of a binding or obligatoryvalid norm.

Thus, while the command or the imperative are the expression of a desire, the norm is the expression of a duty, of an "Ought" (*Sollen*). Let us now see in more detail how the relations between the imposed behavior and the consequence linked to its disrespect are fixed in the formulation of a legal norm.

3.3.2 *Causality x Imputation*

Another term belonging to the legal terminology and finding an echo in History of philosophy appears when they we confronted to affirmations of the form: "All norms are valid merely conditionally", or also: "The general norms of positive morality and positive law are always hypothetical". In the present section we will analyze the notion of *condition* as it is expressed in the formulation of norms.

Certainly, all positive norms link a behavior as obligatory or as forbidden under certain circumstances. In the same way, when a norm prescribes a sanction, this sanction is seen to be the consequence of the illegal act also expressed in the norm. This comes on the (very simplified) form of "If someone commits an illegal act, then a sanction ought to be applied to this person".

In Philosophy, conditional sentences are logically evaluated by a logical connective called the *material conditional*, which has the particularity of not specifying a causal relationship between the antecedent and the consequent. In Logic, the "if ... then" construction will only be false when the antecedent is true at the same time as the consequent is false. So, the sentence "If A, B" is false when A is true and B is false. All other combinations render the sentence true, what yields a lot of bizarre consequences when we leave the formal level. For example, any material conditional with a true consequent is true, and any material conditional sentence with a false antecedent is also true (for example, "If I'm 10 feet tall, I play basketball with my Martians friends on Saturdays").

Given this context, when we say, together with Kelsen, that the legal norms are expressed on the form of "If A is, then B ought to be", then how is this supposed be comprehended under a philosophical perspective?

Conditional legal norms cannot be treated as conditional sentences because the link between the antecedent and the consequent is not linking two facts from the "Is" realm. What makes the connection between antecedent and consequent in a legal norm belongs to the realm of Law, the normative or the "Ought" domain, and the relation is then called a relation of *imputation*.

The main difference between imputation and causality is that the imputation link needs to be created, it has to be produced by a specific act of will for each and every norm, while the causal link is completely independent from an agent. The causal link is what is expressed, for example, on the rules studied by the natural sciences, such as the laws of physics, for instance. In this sense, the laws of physics will continue to be true even if people don't know about them or would stop believing them: they are autonomous in this sense, they are "self-governing". On the contrary, legal norms are always the product of the human arbitrary will. In this sense, the apparent "normativity" involved in the context of those natural laws doesn't really express that something *ought to be* the case, but they rather manifest some kind of "regularity" or patterns that are systematized in and by the science.

So, in the imputation, there is no relation of necessity between antecedent and consequent, because the link between the two states of affairs is always dependent on someone's will or decision. Consequently, in the norm "If someone commits a murder, he/she ought to be submitted to criminal imprisonment", no necessity link is present, since the existence of the norm doesn't avoid the fact that there are murders who are not put in prison. The "Ought" link, once differentiated from the "is" link, that is, the duality between causality and imputation, characterizes the methodological abyss which drastically separates those two domains.

3.4 **Fictions**

For a person who is interested in the study of theories of law, but who does not have a formal legal background, some particular kinds of normative formulations can seem to be very confusing. Let us take the example given by Prof. Otto Pfersmann, when he talks about a somehow "polemical"[31] issue: legal fictions. Let us see the example, when Prof. Pfersmann expresses the following norm:

> *"Only women have access to this swimming-pool, the man working as swimming teacher is a woman in the sense of this statute."* [32]

It seems strange to believe that this could actually be a valid norm. But this example shows precisely the complete independence of the notion of *validity* in relation to what some would say to be its correspondent: the notion of *truth*. In this example, the norm can be a valid one, even if its content presents an impossible state of affairs, namely, a man to be a woman. This norm is nevertheless perfectly understandable for their addressees (after an interpretation); it can be, and actually it is respected by them in the same way that it can also be violated by its addressees.

But these cases, where the fiction regards a – normally, contradictory – element present in the linguistic formulation of the norm, i.e., in its very

---

[31] The topic regarding legal fictions is an especially interesting one. But, unfortunately, a difficulty one can find in approaching this matter from a philosophical point of view (in the context of conferences or discussions with the Law professionals) is that there is a general hesitation from the part of the jurists to grasp how problematic and arbitrary the application of legal fictions can appear to be under a rigorous theoretical perspective. This is in part due to the fact that legal fictions are also highly "efficient" in the legal practice, which can give the wrong idea that their application is always theoretically sound. Many problems can be raised on the topic of legal fictions from a philosophical or logical perspective, and a whole thesis could be written by philosophers interested only in that matter. The reluctance between the two fields regarding an open discussion on this specific topic could then, perhaps, be put aside. Due to this context, we will retain the discussion in this study to the notion of Basic Norm solely, and not in the legal fictions in general.
[32] Pfersmann, O. (2004, p. 43). The passage is a personal translation from the original in French.

content, are not what interests Kelsen and the theory he proposes. Kelsen is not interested in norms containing fictions in their formulation, but rather in norms which are, themselves, of fictive nature. The presence of fictions in the kelsenian theory is represented by the notion of *Basic Norm*, which is, in the *General Theory of Norms*, considered to be an example of fiction by excellence.

But, before approaching the notion itself, it's important to understand how norms are "organized" in a positivist legal system.

3.4.1 *The hierarchy of norms*

Now that we explained that norms are valid when they are the objective meaning of an act of will, let us see in detail how this normative creation happens.

Norms can be general of individual. Kelsen explains the difference between them in a very clear manner:

> "A norm is individual if it decrees a once-only individually specified instance of behavior to be obligatory. For example, the judicial decision that Schulze the thief is to be imprisoned for one year. A norm is general if it decrees some generally specified behavior to be obligatory. For instance, the norm that all thieves are to be imprisoned."[33]

---

[33] Kelsen, H. (1979, p.7).

The content of such norms are always a determined human behavior[34], i.e., the behavior rendered obligatory by the norm. In this sense, it's not entirely correct to say that a *norm* is obligatory, because it is, instead, the *behavior* (actions or omissions) that is made obligatory by the norm. By this perspective, individual norms are observed directly by the addressees, while the general norms are observed only indirectly by them.

But the relation between the two kinds of norm is a direct "dependency" relation: the general norm with corresponding content must be recognized as present in the legal order in question (i.e., as "posited" or "written down" by the Legislator) so that the individual norm can be created by the Judge for the specific case. Each individual norm needs its own act of will from the Judge.

In this sense the individual norm must be grounded by a content-correspondent general norm. Even if this process represents somehow an "individualization" of the general norm, no deduction relation is established, since, as we've just mentioned, the Judge needs to enact a brand new act of will whose meaning will be the validity of the individual norm. Without this second act of meaning, now coming from the Judge, and which is completely separated from the act of will of the Legislator concerning the general norm, no new legal norm is legitimately created.

So, even if there exists a logical relation between the descriptions of the behaviors serving as content in both general and individual norms (they are correspondent), there is no logical relation between the validity of those two norms; i.e. between their existence. The individual norm will only be valid if

---

[34] We will approach the problem or the relation between form and content in the legal norm in the chapter dedicated to the study of the notion of practical syllogism (Chapters 9 and 10).

enacted by an authorized person, if it will be the objective meaning of his/her act of will.

In this perspective, in order to give a general structure to the legal system, one can consider the general norm as being in a "higher" position compared to that of the individual norm, giving to this "lower" norm the reason for its validity (together with the act of will of the Judge). Normally this structure is represented by a "pyramid" of norms, where the individual norms serve as the basis.

The notion of *Stufenbau* is presented in the *Pure Theory of Law* and it's taken for granted in the following writings, especially in the *General Theory of Norms*, where it is barely even mentioned. Nevertheless, this notion remains one of the most popular concepts of Kelsen's legal theory, i.e., it will mark Kelsen's approach against Hart's perspective of the normative order according to different levels (primary and secondary legal rules – being the latest represented by the rules of recognition, of change and of adjudication) as well as against other more contemporary approaches considering the legal or moral orders as a complex normative web.

In this sense, in order to answer to the question whether a given norm is a binding legal norm, we have to consider two aspects: whether the content of the norm is grounded by a previous – higher – norm and whether the person enacting the norm is authorized – also by a higher competence norm, giving him/her the power to do so. The search for this grounding for the normative validity should then meet an end when we arrive at the Constitution of a country, for example. But then the further question still arises: "Which legal norm gave to the Legislator of the first Constitution of a country the power, the authorization to enact it as a valid set of norms?" There is no higher norm to ground it, no further element. Kelsen will suggest that it can only be the *presupposition* of a higher norm that enables the normative chain constituting the *Stufenbau*.

3.4.2 The Basic Norm (Grundnorm)

The notion of Basic Norm is one of the more intricate in legal theory. Since this norm is not actually posited, it cannot be said to be valid in the same sense as all the other "ordinary" norms composing the system, or to exist in the same way that they do, otherwise it would also have to be present in the legal system, right above the Constitution, on the very top of the pyramid, which would, again, perpetuate the problem of the lacking of a higher norm to justify its own validity.

Kelsen argues that the Basic norm is a merely thought norm, i.e. it is the sense of a fictive act of will. The Basic Norm should then be seen, as we will argue in the special chapter we dedicated to the study of this notion[35], as a methodological apparatus serving to give the formal justification of the validity of the Constitution (and, subsequently, of the legal system as a whole). Despite still having to be regarded as a norm (where the needing of the fictional element comes from), this "norm" has a pure epistemological function: without it, the collection of legal norms could not be seen as a coherent normative system capable of being rationally described. It is only under the presupposition of the Basic Norm that legal science can perform its function.

---

[35] Cf. Chapter 6.

The notion of Basic Norm was invented by Kelsen and severely criticized by his contemporaries. The legal positivist Herbert Hart himself has strongly attacked the notion as being an unnecessary normative "duplication" and needless "complication" for the study of legal positivism. For Hart, the abidingness of the constitution is simply rendered evident by his "rule of recognition". Differently from Kelsen's perspective, Hart established a meta-level for the rules of recognition permitting to recognize what is binding Law, to check if the steps on normative creation were correctly taken (i.e. if the normative creation procedure was correctly followed) to justify legal validity. However, Kelsen tries to avoid this upper separated level of secondary rules in order to be able to keep positive law itself as the only source of law (*Stufenbau*), preserving also the notion of "purity". Hart's normative perspective grounded on the notion of rule of recognition clearly does not perform in the same way. Some of the differences are that:

> *"(…) because the rule of recognition is a social rule, it is capable of being an ultimate rule. It is ultimate in the sense that it does not exist in virtue of any other rule. Its existence is secured simply because of its acceptance and practice. The primary rules of the legal system, by contrast, are not ultimate because they exist in virtue of the rule of recognition. The rule of recognition validates, but is not itself validated."*[36]

Nevertheless, this approach contains its own difficulties concerning, for example, the possible linguistic formulations of these rules of recognition, or even their relation with the naturalistic fallacy, since it grounds legal validity

---

[36] Shapiro, S. J. (2009, p. 5).

in some kind of social commonly-known "standard" practice, i.e., in the simple factual recognition of their authority.

The notion of Basic Norm might be more complex, but it seems fitter to meet the purposes on establishing a general theory for legal positivism, since it preserves the theses and precepts of the positivist tradition, which is not the case of Hart's approach, at least considering the hybrid conception of his rule of recognition.

Kelsen, very didactically, give us a very fine example, this time coming from the field of positive morals instead of the legal field, that might help us explaining the place and function of the Basic Norm in a positive normative system:

> "For example: Paul comes home from school and says to his father: 'My classmate Hugo is my enemy, I hate him.' Thereupon, Paul's father addresses an individual norm to him: 'You are to love your enemy Hugo and not hate him.' Paul asks his father: 'Why am I to love my enemy?', that is, he asks why the subjective meaning of he's father's act of will is also its objective meaning, why it is a norm binding on him, or – and this is the same question – he wants to know the reason for the validity of this norm. Whereupon his father says: 'Because Jesus commanded "Love your enemies".' Paul then asks 'Why is anyone to obey the commands of Jesus?'; that is, he asks why the subjective meaning of Jesus's act of will is also its objective meaning, why it is a valid norm, or – and this is the same question – what is the reason for the validity of this general norm. The only possible answer to that is: Because as a Christian one presupposes that one is to

obey the commands of Jesus. This is a statement about the validity of a norm which must be presupposed in the thinking of a Christian in order to found the validity of the norms of Christian morality. It is the Basic Norm of Christian morality, and it founds the validity of all the norms of Christian morality. It is a 'basic' norm, because nothing further can be asked about the reason for its validity. It is not a positive norm (i.e. posited by a real act of will) but a norm presupposed in the thinking of Christians, in other words, it is a fictitious norm."[37]

The tricky relations between norms and sentences about their validity on the context of the presupposition of the Basic Norm need a more refined treatment, which will be delivered in the chapter concerning the notion of Fiction in legal positivism[38].

3.5 Normative Conflicts and Logical Contradictions

The interest of Kelsen in the problem of the applicability of logic to norms is marked by two main questions that can be seen as instantiations of the general problem of the applicability, namely:

1 – Could the principle of non-contradiction be applied to a situation of conflict between legal or between moral norms?

---
[37] Kelsen, H. (1979, p.254).
[38] Cf. Chapter 6.

2 – Could the procedure for the normative creation be expressed in a syllogism, and be ruled by the rules of inference?

In the present section, we will analyze (1), leaving (2) for the next, following section of this chapter.[39]

3.5.1 *The problem of applicability*

If we start the story by its ending, we can yet announce that Kelsen completely denies the possibility of application of traditional bivalent logic to norms. The main argument will depart from the fact that traditional logic can only be applied to true/false propositions – that is, it presupposes truth values –, and the whole Kelsenian argumentation will be focused precisely on expressing the differences between a valid norm and those true/false propositions. This approach is also corroborated by Kelsen's previous theses concerning the non-reducibility or non-deduction between the realms of "Is" and "Ought", as well as the differences between acts of will and acts of thought and, of course, the preservation of the "purity" as a methodological precept.

The position Kelsen takes with regard to the problem of the relations between Law and Logic is clearly dependent upon his own definition of what a positive valid norm is. In this context, Kelsen is trying to remove the focus from the possible deduction – in the case of normative creation – or comparison – in the case of normative conflict – between the normative *contents*. He then tries to put the focus on the problem of the relations

---

[39] Cf. Section 3.6.

between the *validity* of the norms, that is, their legitimate existence. In this sense, we should face the problem with regard to how those logical principles act on the *validity* of the norms in situation of conflict or in the process of normative creation.

The point is that the validity is directly linked to the *act of will* positing the norm. This relation cannot be grasped by logic, since it consist in a matter of the willing of an agent, an intentional act arbitrary upon someone's will towards someone else's behavior. This last aspect is outside the scope of the rules or principles of logic.

But let us go step by step and first consider how Kelsen deals specifically with the case of legal normative conflicts, considering its possibility of being treated by the principle of non-contradiction:

3.5.2 *Conflicts between Norms*

Concerning the definition of the normative conflict, it is important to note, from the very beginning, that the situation of conflict is "located" in the legal modality concerning the behavior contained in the norm. Professor Uta Bindreiter gives a clear explanation and an example as it follows:

> "(a norm conflict) is extant where the one norm renders a certain form of behavior as obligatory, while the other norm renders obligatory a form of behavior incompatible with the first.
> Consider, for example, the following two norms, addressed to one and the same norm subject:

> Norm 1. Peter shall do A at 3 p.m. today.
>
> Norm 2. Peter shall forbear from doing A at 3 p.m. today.
>
> While norm 1 prescribes act A, norm 2 prescribes the forbearance therefrom, that is, forbids the doing of A. Consequently, whatever Peter does (which includes his being completely passive), he will inevitably violate one or the other of these norms."[40]

The main point to be stressed when defining normative conflicts is that both norms need to be valid. In the same way, the sentences formulated by legal science describing the validity of those norms will both be evaluated as true.

According to the terminology we've been using in our study so far, we can also recognize that, while the norms are the meaning of acts of will, the sentences are the meaning or the expression of acts of thought. The interest in stressing this aspect becomes clear when we notice that, in the case of two contradictory sentences, one is evaluated as true and the other as false. Also, the means to deal with normative conflicts is normally by derogation, when the validity of one of the norms is abolished. But, in the case of the contradictory sentences, one of them is false from the very beginning: the principle of non-contradiction does not "change" or "abolish" the sentences' truth values.

As the fact that contradictory sentences and conflicting norms have no similarities becomes more and more clear, it becomes also necessary to deeply analyze how Law deals with the situation of conflict, i.e., how the

---

[40] Bindreiter, U. (2002, p.135)

abolishment of one of the norms' validity is performed, so that the conflict is solved.

By preserving the notion of "purity", Kelsen is interested in showing that no external element is needed for the treatment of these "internal problems" of the legal domain, which may eventually arise within the normative systems. But the main point is that law has its own way to deal with the normative conflicts, let us see how:

3.5.3 *Derogation*

Derogation is not a principle in the same way as the logical principle of non-contradiction. It cannot even be called a special *legal* principle. Derogation is one of the normative functions among others (permitting, forbidding, empowering...). The derogation norm is created by the legal authority only when in presence of a situation of conflict. This means that the derogation norm is not one of the two norms in conflict, but a third norm. In this sense, it can be called a "dependent" norm regarding the norms in conflict: the derogation norm has its own validity as dependent on the validity of the norm it is supposed to repeal.

Thus, this derogation norm is not directed to the behavior of people with the intention to regulate it, as the other norms of the legal order. Rather, it is directed towards the validity of one of the norms in conflict, with the intention to abolish its existence. Therefore, the derogation norm cannot be observed neither effective, nor even violated in the same sense as the other "regular" norms. In order to introduce the concept of derogation, Kelsen uses again an example of positive Morals, showing that is not only in the situation of normative conflict that this norm can take place and be used by the authority of the normative system in question:

> "It can also occur in a positive morality: for example, in Christian morality, when Jesus says: 'Ye have heard that it hath been said, Thou shalt love thy neighbor, and hate thine enemy. But I say unto you, Love your enemies...' (Matt. 5:43-4). That means, I repeal the validity of the norm 'Hate your enemies' and I posit the norm 'Love your enemies'. The repeal of the validity of the old norms and the positing of the new norm are two different acts, which must be kept apart in the exposition of the morality in question."[41]

Another aspect that is also important to notice is how misleading the legal principle of Roman law saying that *Lex posteriori derogate priori*[42] is, when it gives the idea that it is one of the two conflicting norms (namely, the "newer" or more recent norm) that abolishes the validity of the former, older norm. This legal principle is very common and indeed very useful in legal practice, and it actually works as a presupposition in the mind of the Judge. With the derogation norm it is similar: it is not permanently present in the legal order amongst the other "regular" norms, but is taken for granted by the Judge when he/she is confronted with a case of normative conflict. The derogation norm, as well as the principle *Lex posteriori derogate priori*, is tacitly regarded as self-evident depending on the case in question, and framed by the liberty

---

[41] Kelsen, H. (1979, p. 106).
[42] The same is valid concerning also the principle "*Lex specialis derogate lege generali*". A fine analysis of those principles in the context of conflicts is given by Kammerhofer, J. (2005).

of interpretation of the Judge. We consider its validity only as long as it is directed to the validity of the norm-to-be-abolished, knowing that it will lose it at the same time as the norm it abolishes.

3.5.4 *Temporality and Efficacy*

Another case in which the norm might lose its validity by derogation – besides the situation of conflict – is when a norm stops being observed by its addressees or applied by Law, i.e., when it loses its *efficacy* with the time.

Efficacy is a term belonging to the indicative, factual level of what "Is", because it is directly linked to the *fact* of the observance of a norm or the application of this norm's sanction (punishment). Since general norms, according to Kelsen, are formulated by linking a sanction to the disrespect of the behavior prescribed, the norm can be in this sense observed either by the "citizens", for example, as well as by the legal organs which have to apply the sanctions. In the same way, it can lose it efficacy when it stops being either observed and/or applied when it's violated.

An example of a norm which has lost its efficacy by no longer being observed was the Prohibition in the United States, concerning the sale, production, importation, and transportation of alcoholic beverages, which remained valid from 1920 to 1933.[43] The general increasing of disrespect to the law with the passing of the years (allied to the development of the black market concerning the sale of alcohol, together with the crash of 1929 and the

---

[43] Curiously enough, the *consumption* of alcohol was never prohibited during this period.

following Great Depression), lead to movements asking for its repeal. Finally, the law was formally derogated in 1933.

On the other hand, the lacking of application of the sanction is also determinant. For instance, an interesting fact is that, until a couple of years ago (2013), women were legally forbidden to wear trousers in the city of Paris, in France. The law, which dates back to 1799, *"required women to ask police for special permission to 'dress as men' in Paris, or risk being taken into custody. In 1892 and 1909 the rule was amended to allow women to wear trousers, 'if the woman is holding a bicycle handlebar or the reins of a horse'."*[44] Of course, this law was not being enforced during the last decades and, probably for that reason, or at least directly related to that reason, women also stop observing it with the passing of time[45]. But, formally, the law only stops existing in the legal documents after its derogation. That's what happened regarding this law in 2013, after the strong insistence of Mme. Najat Vallaud-Belkacem, France's minister of women's rights at the time. But one has to recognize that, formally and legally, until the year of 2013, that law was still a legitimate valid law within the territory of the city of Paris.

With those examples we can see how, in the end, the validity of a norm – its existence – is influenced by the notion of efficacy. We can say that a norm, in order to *remain* valid, must be minimally – "by and large" – efficient. This represent a serious problem in the sense that it "blurs" the limits between

---

[44] Seen in March 2015 at:
http://www.telegraph.co.uk/news/worldnews/europe/france/9845545/Women-in-Paris-finally-allowed-to-wear-trousers.html

[45] It is actually hard to fix a causal relation: the women stop observing the law because it was not being systematically applied anymore? Or is it the authorities who stop applying the sanction because the women stop observing the Law? The answer is vague because the lack of efficacy doesn't happen from one day to another. It takes years, even decenies to observe the looseness of the relation between the lacking of observance and the lacking of application.

"Is" and "Ought" and takes the form of a naturalistic fallacy, when the validity seems to be reduced to the notion of efficacy.

This major problem was recognized by Kelsen himself, who tries to somehow minimize it as he defends that the efficacy would be a *condition* for legal validity, without being the *reason* for it. He illustrates this thesis with a clever metaphor: *"Just as the facts of being born and being fed are conditions for human life without themselves being life, so the fact of being posited and being effective are conditions for the validity of a norm without themselves being validity."*[46]

3.6 Practical Reasoning and the Rule of Inference

Besides the case of normative conflicts, another context where Kelsen considers the problem of the applicability of logic to norms is that of normative creation, i.e., where an individual legal norm is created by the Judge.

This question can be formulated in a broader sense, including not only legal norms, but also moral norms and even "ordinary" imperatives. It consists then in the classical problem of practical syllogisms, where norms are present in the premises and/or in the conclusion of a syllogism.

> *People should love their enemies.*
>
> *John is your enemy.*
> _____
>
> *Therefore, you should love John.*

---

[46] Kelsen, H. (1979, p.140).

Actually, as soon as we abandon the strictly legal field, we are able to remark how difficult it would be to argue against the apparent validity of practical syllogisms as the abovementioned. Nevertheless, the problem is that in the example above, we are "inadvertently" mixing, and therefore taken for granted to correlation and even the identification of the truth value of a sentence with the validity of a legal or moral norm[47].

Besides all of the differences we already mentioned about sentences and norms, one of them is of fundamental importance in the present context:

The statement or sentence[48] is the meaning of an act of thought. The norm is the meaning of an act of will. Each act of will can "generate" one and only one norm. This means that the norm in the conclusion of the syllogism cannot be derived from the norm in the major premise, because it still needs its "own" act of will which is different and independent from the factual act of will "generating" the norm in the major premise.

Thus, even if the content expressed by the norm in the conclusion is somehow correlated to the content of the norm representing the first premise of the syllogism, it is still not possible to establish any kind of logical relation between the validity, the specific legal existence of those two norms. We need a brand new factual act of will regarding the norm of the conclusion, and the fact of admitting the possibility of the simple logical deduction would be also ignoring the fact that there is no "authority" positing this new norm and legitimating its existence.

Another way of explain this is by saying that there is no relation of necessity expressed by the inference bar of the syllogism, as well as there is no

---

[47] We beg the reader not to confound legal validity with logical validity.
[48] Kelsen seems to identify the notions of statement and sentence.

preservation of the truth value or of the legal validity, which themselves also have no correlation between them. A valid norm as a major premise and a fact as minor premise won't guarantee the validity of the norm in the conclusion, because its validity is still dependent upon an act of will coming from an authorized person.

Concerning this point we can also perceive a further difference between the legal norms and the statements: while the validity of the legal or moral norm is directly dependent upon one person's act of will, the truth value of the statement is in nothing dependent upon one person's act of thought. This strong dependency relation between the norm and the act of will is expressed by Kelsen with the formula *"no imperative without an imperator, no norm without a norm-positing authority, that is, no norm without an act of will of which it is the meaning"*.[49]

3.6.1 *Dissipating the confusion*

We can explain the apparent "evidence" of the logical validity of the argument by noticing that it may actually come from the fact that the norm has a content which is indeed preserved when passing through the inference bar of the practical syllogism. We know the content of the norm which "is supposed to" be in the conclusion, and that is because of our acts of thought, because of our rational reasoning about the content of the norms.

But still, that is different from enacting a legally binding norm, something which can only be achieved by an act of will, coming from an authorized

---

[49] Kelsen, H. (1979, p. 234).

person. In the case of the "ordinary" imperatives, there is no need of the binding aspect, but there's still the need of a new act of will directed to someone's behavior. The point is that we are not allowed to step into the normative level and assume that our reason is capable of positing norms, of establishing their validity. The recognition of this fact represents not only a refusal and an attack to the notion of practical reasoning, but also to any possible comparison or identification between the outcomes of acts of will (imperatives and norms) and the outcomes of acts of thought (sentences).

Thus, maybe the fact of using the right terminology might help on dissipating the confusion around this misleading notion of practical syllogism. What actually happens when an individual legal norm is created is that the existence, the validity of a general norm is *recognized* (because its presence or not in a determined legal order is indeed a verifiable fact). Then, when in presence of the case to be considered (previously expressed by the minor premise in our example of practical syllogism), the Judge is capable of *positing* an individual norm, via his/her act of will. Only then we have met all the necessary steps for legal normative creation: the validity of a general norm with corresponding content and the act of will from an authorized person.

Last but not least, another issue to be taken into account is that there must be always some place left for the interpretation from the part of the Judge. There is no sense in structuring this creative process in the scheme of a syllogism, since there is no question of preserving of truth values nor legal validity, nor necessity when going from the "recognition" step to the "positing" step.

3.7 Final Remarks on this Topic

The notions briefly presented in this chapter are the ones having a direct influence on the analysis we aim to develop concerning the possible relations between legal positivism and philosophy.

It is straightforward that there are several other legal notions that also deserve a thorough philosophical analyses concerning their interdisciplinary pertinence. But, in our specific case, where we take as background the Kelsenian problematic around the possibility of application of logic to norms, together with the concepts and theses that this author makes use in order to justify his approach, those are the most relevant notions to be analyzed.

So, after this general background of the terminology Kelsen established in order to explain his scientific project concerning the positive legal systems of norms, we are now able to approach each one of those notions separately.

Chapter 4

Legal Positivism: A defense of the Scientific Method

> "The existence of law is one thing;
> its merit or demerit is another."
> John Austin[50]

In this chapter we intend to reinforce the idea of legal positivism as being the most suitable context for a rigorous scientific approach to Law.

Since the general aim of our investigation is to develop a systematic study about the possible relations between Philosophy and the study of norms, it would still seem reasonable to raise objections of the like: "But Philosophy already deals with these problems since its ancient developments!". And that argument is actually fair enough. Besides, Aristotle's moral philosophy, for example, represents an effort to philosophically systematize the rules concerning how people should rightly conduct their behavior in society. In a similar way, the philosophical field of Ethics will analyze the norms of custom (*ethos*) according to concepts of value such as the good, the evil, the just and so on, in order to provide systematized studies about them...

---

[50] Austin, J. (1832, p.157). John Austin is considered to be the founder of legal positivism.

Another interesting aspect of this philosophical context is that it actually seems to find the real correlation of the legal field with the current of Natural law. The Natural law tradition represents a normative system combining both legal and moral elements, i.e., it incorporates moral values (good, just, valuable...) not only as a qualification but also as a criterion to define what a legitimate legal norm is.

Then, the apparently genuine question arises: "Why not taking the Natural Law tradition as the normative context to analyze all of those concepts shared by legal and philosophical fields?"

We answer to this question by pointing to the fact that a legal theory based on Natural law perspective will necessarily have to engage with concepts and thesis that fall outside the scientific frame.

Nevertheless, our contribution to this discussion consists in the attempt to show that the limits between those two schools of thought are less rigidly marked when we consider the positivist theory as an empirical scientific approach for the description of a determined set of positive legal or moral norms. This thesis will be explained in detail in the last section of the present chapter.

4.1 Positivism versus Natural Law Theories

It is common-knowledge among the specialist in the works of Kelsen the fact that we can identify several "phases" in the development of his legal theory[51]. The criteria for this kind of periodization is based on several important aspects of Kelsen's theory as, for example, the influence of the Kantian philosophy over Kelsen's general conceptions or the possible relations between Logic and legal and moral norms[52].

The first chapter of Kelsen's *General Theory of Norms*[53] is dedicated to the definition of norms in the context of the legal positivism. While legal positivism is committed to defining a norm by identifying it with its validity, a more intuitive attempt would maybe establish a correspondence between the notion of norm and the content that is expressed by it, the "something" which is commanded, or forbidden, or permitted. However, this kind of perspective is not proper to the legal positivism, but rather to Natural law approaches, which consider the normative content as making reference to general moral principles that are supposed to be followed.

For an exposition of the concepts developed in the context of legal positivism, a fine mode to proceed may be to compare them with an "opposite" context such as the school of legal naturalism. In this sense, we will try to display at what length the concepts belonging to those two different approaches to law may still be obscure and hide problems on their very own fields.

To start with it, as we have already seen, Kelsen develops his entire "pure" legal theory in the frame of legal Positivism, which historically opposes itself to the Natural law tradition. Even inside the tradition of positivism, Kelsen offers a new methodology, based on this concept of "purity", since he himself

---

[51] The periodization of Kelsen's legal theory is a very polemic issue. For the most important attempts and for an overview of the divergences, cf. Paulson, S. (1998) and Paulson, S. (1999), but also Heidemann, C. (1997) and Bulygin, E. (1990).
[52] For a rigorous analysis of the specific problem of the applicability of Logic to the normative field according to three different phases, cf. Sievers, J. (2009).
[53] Kelsen, H. (1979).

attacks his positivist predecessors by denouncing their tendency of "old-fashioned" positivism, by identifying the norm with a fact, for example. For legal positivists, every norm belonging to a legal system, and once enacted by a legal authority, is a *valid* norm. This comes in contrast with the identification of the norm with an abstract moral principle, as it was done by natural law scholars. Kelsen, in his turn, defends a rather unusual definition of Law, namely, that "Law is Norm". This claim is related to the well-known saying making Kelsen's enthusiastic devotion to the principle of purity much known at his times: "Norm is Norm"[54], Kelsen says. This statement, despite the fact of being a simple tautology, is immediately understood by anyone implicated on the issues of the "defense" of legal positivism: the definition of norm must be given without any reference to elements exterior to the legal field itself.

But, in order to better understand the relation between Natural Law and Positivism when trying to give a fair definition of what a norm is, let us go back in time and analyze the first tensions regarding this definition in this classical passage concerning a dialogue between Pericles and Alcibiades, described in Xenophon's *Memorabilia*:

> "It is said that Alcibiades, before he was twenty, had a conversation with Pericles, his guardian and the head of the Athenian state, on the subject of the Law.
> 'Tell me, Pericles,' Alcibiades asked, 'can you explain to me what a law is?'
> 'Of course I can,' answered Pericles.

---

[54] Hart, H. (1998, p. 70). Concerning this saying of Kelsen, the whole passage of Hart making reference to it worth being quoted: "... towards the end of our debate, when upon Kelsen emphasizing in stentorian tones, so remarkable in an octogenarian (or in any one), that 'Norm is Norm' and not something else, I was so startled that I (literally) fell over backwards in my chair."

'Then please do so,' said Alcibiades. 'For when I hear people praised for being law-abiding, I am of the opinion that no man can rightly be praised in this way if he does not know what a law is.'

'What you want is nothing difficult, Alcibiades – to know what a law is. All these are laws, all that the people in assembly approve and enact, setting out what is or is not to be done.'

'With the idea that good is to be done, or bad?'

'Of course good is to be done, my boy, not bad!' Pericles declared.

'But if it is not the people, if, as in an oligarchy, it is a minority who assemble and enact what is or is not to be done, what are these?'

'Everything the ruling power in the state enacts with due deliberation, enjoining what is to be done, is called a law,' intoned Pericles.

'Then if a despot, being the ruling power in the state, enacts what the citizens are to do, is this, too, a law?'

'Yes, everything a despot, as ruler, enacts,' answered Pericles, 'this, too, is called a law.'

'But what is force, the negation of law, Pericles? Is it not when the stronger compels the weaker to do his will, not by persuasion but by force?'

'Yes, that is my opinion,' agreed Pericles.

'Then everything a despot enacts and compels the citizens to do, without persuasion, is the negation of law?'

> 'Correct,' said Pericles. 'I retract my statement that everything a despot enacts is a law, for without persuasion, his enactments are not law.'
>
> 'And what the minority enact, not by persuading the majority but through superior power, are we or are we not to call it force?'
>
> 'I believe', answered Pericles, 'that without persuasion, whatever one compels another to do – whether by enactment or otherwise – is force rather than law.'
>
> 'Then whatever the people as a whole enact, not by persuasion but by being stronger than the owners of property, this, too, would be force rather than law?'
>
> 'Let me tell you, Alcibiades, when I was your age I, too, was good at this sort of thing. We used to practice just the sort of clever quibbling I think you are practicing right now.'
>
> 'How I should like to have known you in those days, Pericles, when you were in your prime!'"[55]

Thus, when Pericles ends up admitting that "law is simply an institutionalized expression of the existing power relations", he suddenly seems to recognize how strange and difficult it would be to have to defend such a claim, and ends up admitting that it actually might not be so.

But the only reason that leads Pericles to decline from the claim that *law is what the despot enacts* is some kind of "intrinsic" belief supported by a moral background. The morality aspect seems in this example to be clearly linked with the notion of "persuasion": the citizens must not to be forced; instead,

---

[55] Calhoun quoting Xenophon's Memorabilia, I. ii. 40-6 (1944, p. 78-80).

there must be some sort of concordance and consensus over the law. Therefore, while the initial intention of Pericles in the dialog is directed to a definition of Law separating the legal field from morality (namely, by defending that the Law is the simple expression of institutionalized power), Alcibiades seems, in his turn, to defend that this definition must be explained in terms of morals in order to make sense or to be able to be generally accepted.

Moreover, when regarding Natural law specifically, Aristotle's *Rethoric* gives us a definition based on the same kind of perspective. He makes reference to Sophocles' Antigone, namely in the passage where the sister buries her brother, something which, at those times, was consider to be against the law. Nevertheless, the sister defends herself by saying that she based her action in a higher law, a just law, something like "a law from above". Aristotle explains:

> "We may begin by observing that they have been defined relatively to two kinds of law, and also relatively to two classes of persons. By the two kinds of law I mean particular law and universal law. Particular law is that which each community lays down and applies to its own members: this is partly written and partly unwritten. Universal law is the law of Nature. For there really is, as every one to some extent divines, a natural justice and injustice that is binding on all men, even on those who have no association or covenant with each other. It is this that Sophocles' Antigone clearly means when she says that the burial of Polyneices was a just

act in spite of the prohibition: she means that it was just by nature."[56]

Those two examples show the intuitional difficulty in separating the legal filed from the moral one. Then, in those cases, to give a definition of what a legitimate legal norm would be tends to always point to the fact that its fair or goodness-directed content must be something to be taken into account.

4.1.1 Legal Validity and the Positive Law Perspective

Kelsen's theory of Law is a theory about the legal knowledge, the object being the norm itself. In order to know and define what a legal norm is, we must isolate it from any external element which we normally would associate with it, namely, justice, efficacy, sociological aspects, as well as from the disciplines that could somehow be related, such as sociology, psychology or ethics. Surely the field of Law involves all those aspects in its everyday practice, but the point is that those elements must be excluded from the study and comprehension of law itself.

Concerning Ethics specifically, Kelsen insists that *"the purity of the theory is to be secured against the claims of the natural law theory, which... takes legal theory out of the realm of positive legal norms and into the realm of ethico-political postulates"*[57]. Thus, concerning the definition of Law, Kelsen develops a particular approach to the investigation, turning the question to:

---

[56] Aristotle. Rethoric. Book 1: Chapter 13. [1373b]
[57] Kelsen, H. (1923, p. v).

"How is positive law *qua* object of cognition, *qua* object of cognitive legal science, possible?", which is a very Kantian oriented perspective that marks one of Kelsen's most important and famous works, the *Pure Theory of Law*.

Professor Stanley Paulson, one of the most important, if not *the* most important expert of Kelsen's theory in present times, interprets Kelsen's aims regarding the nature of that theory as the following:

> "In putting his transcendental question Kelsen is not asking whether we cognize legal material, whether we know certain legal propositions to be true. Rather, he assumes that we have such knowledge, and is asking how we can have it. To capture something of the peculiarly transcendental twist to Kelsen's question, we might ask: given that we know something to be true, what presupposition is at work? More specifically, what presupposition is at work without which the proposition that we know to be true could not be true?"[58]

The answer clearly point to Kelsen's intricate theory of the basic norm, which we shall not discuss in length in this chapter[59], but which will nevertheless help us to understand Kelsen's differentiation between Static and Dynamic principles ruling the normative systems of positivism.

4.1.2 *Static versus Dynamics*

---

[58] Paulson, S. (1992, p.312).
[59] Cf. chapter 6.

Legal positivism identifies the norm with the normative validity, and not with its content. Consider the following passage from Bruno Celano:

> "According to Kelsen, validity is binding force. A norm has binding force if and only if it ought to be complied with (obeyed). Saying that a norm ought to be obeyed amounts to saying that one ought to behave as the norm prescribes. So, for instance, asserting that the norm 'Children ought to obey their parents' is valid amounts to asserting that children ought to do what the norm prescribes them to do. What the norm prescribes them to do is, however, to obey their parents. Asserting that the norm 'Children ought to obey their parents' is valid, amounts, therefore, to asserting that children ought to obey their parents. Generally speaking, whoever asserts that a norm 'Op', is valid is at the same time asserting that Op, and vice versa (the statement "The norm 'Op' is valid" entails – and is entailed by – the statement 'Op'). On Kelsen's conception of validity, therefore, asserting that a given norm is valid amounts to (is logically equivalent to) asserting – i.e. iterating, accepting, endorsing, assenting to, the norm itself."[60]

This long passage also illustrates a very basic thesis of Kelsen, namely, the one saying that the validity is not a property of the norm in the same way as the truth or falseness are a property of the indicative statement. For Kelsen, the validity is identified with the norm, with its existence as such. This

---

[60] Celano, B. (2000, p. 178).

important aspect gives rise to a remarkable consequence: to give a definition of norm, to explain what is a legal norm equals to explain why the norm is valid, i. e., to justify the validity of the norm. This procedure leads us to investigate the process by which a legal norm is created.

Since positive legal systems are regulated by the principle of self-production and auto-regulation, a norm must be created only when the act of will in question makes reference to another previous valid norm. This process amounts to a regress which ends with a norm whose validity is not based in a previous norm, which according to Kelsen can only be the Basic Norm. Nevertheless, the support and foundation on a previous normative validity is still a necessary but not sufficient step for the normative creation: there's also a need for the unavoidable act of will of an authoritative figure representing the Law, whose objective meaning will be the norm. This additional fundamental step illustrates the importance of the notion of *power* or *authority* in the context of legal positivism.

Thus, it is now clear that to understand what Law is, i.e., whether a prescription is a norm or not, is to give a justification of its validity. Let us illustrate the searching for normative justification by giving an example coming from the field of Literature: in the case of *Sophie's Choice*[61], for instance, the command from the German officer to Sophie, forcing her to choose which one of her two children would be sent to the gas chamber and which one would proceed to the labor camp: is it a valid norm? What makes it binding (obligatory) to the addressee, to Sophie? In the context of legal positivism, despite its bizarre and abnormal substance, it is not the normative content which defines the validity or the abidingness of the norm. According

---

[61] Styron, W. (1979).

to the precepts of positivism, the officer is indeed entitled to enact such a command; he is authorized to enact this as a valid norm addressed to Sophie.

To Kelsen, at least in the *Pure Theory of Law*, normative systems can be classified as dynamic or static. In a static normative system, the due behavior of the individuals is derived from the normative content. The validity of such a norm is then based on the content of a more general valid norm, and the regression goes until the most general principle serving as the content of the most abstract norm funding a normative system. This kind of system is exemplified by moral systems, and an example of the "most general principle" could be the Table of the Ten Commandments in the case of Catholic religion, for instance. The Sacred Table is regarded as "containing in itself" the content to be in all the other derived religious/moral norms, that is, all the other possible norms have to have a content in accord to this general principle in order to be legitimated, in order to be considered as "a part of" that specific moral system. To Kelsen, at least in its early phase, Christian Religion and other positive moral systems represent normative systems ruled by the static principle. This aspect also helps explaining why, in religion or morality, we are normally our own "Judges", that is, there is no need of an authority to posit each one of the individual norms regulating and motivating one's behavior. We only consider the general posited principles and shape our own behavior according to them.

But in a normative system ruled by a dynamic principle, the basic norm funding the legal order provides no content to be derived, but only the attribution of legislative competence for the creation of new norms. The basic norm here only provides the grounding for the validity of the succeeding norms, and it is directed to the authority enacting the norms, by delegating a power. In this dynamic process, no specific content is transmitted along the chain of delegation, and the result of this purely formal process of rule producing is the astonishing fact that any content can be a normative content, since the criteria ultimately lies in the authoritative figure. To Kelsen, positive legal systems are the perfect example of this kind of dynamic mode of operation:

> "The norm system that presents itself as a legal order has essentially a dynamic character. A legal norm is not valid because it has a certain content, that is, because its content is logically deducible from a presupposed basic norm, but because it is created in a certain way – ultimately in a way determined by a presupposed basic norm. For this reason alone does the legal norm belong to the legal order whose norms are created according to this a basic norm. Therefore any kind of content might be law. There is no human behavior which, as such, is excluded from being the content of a legal norm. The validity of a legal norm may not be denied for being (in its content) in conflict with that of another norm which does not belong to the legal order whose basic norm is the reason for the validity of the norm in question. The basic norm of a legal order is not a material norm which, because its content is regarded as immediately self-evident, is presupposed as the highest norm and from which norms for human behavior are logically deduced. The norms of a legal order must be created by a specific process."[62]

---

[62] Kelsen, H. (1960, p. 198).

4.1.3 *Normative Content and the Natural Law Perspective*

Positive Law can fairly be defined as "a system which prescribes the rules of its own development"[63]. Meanwhile, an even much generalized definition can be traced considering natural Law:

> "The first and most abstract notion that can be called 'natural law' is that human beings are a certain kind of being, and the features of that being should direct our understanding of how human beings should live. This approach implies the existence of some sort of objective moral law knowable through reason. It is implicit in what are perhaps the most basic intuitions giving rise to natural law, namely, the sense that there must be some general standard in light of which it is possible to judge human laws or conventions. The classic instance of this idea is found in Sophocles' Antigone, in which a sister disobeys a law by burying her brother, and claims a warrant in higher law for so doing."[64]

For the Thomist perspective of natural law, the evidence of a moral oriented principle guiding the creation and justification of the norms is even stronger:

> "...what to the Thomist is the basic, primary and self-evident principle of the natural law (...) is variously phrased as: follow your nature; act according to your proper end; maintain order; act for your rational end in conformity with your total

---
[63] Silving, H. (1955, p. 489).
[64] Wolfe, C. (2003, p.38).

> nature; bring your essential being to completion; follow your rational inclinations; do good and avoid evil (meaning what is good and bad in light of human nature), etc. In other words, act according to reason."[65]

These passages only reinforce the fact of Legal Positivism and Natural law as having a long history of conflict in legal Philosophy. The main argument of Natural law defenders points to the necessity of a moral grounding for the norms: a norm, in order to be valid, must be a fair norm, a quality which is achieved by the derivation from a general principle given by God or Nature or, due to its evidence, by Rationality. This claim covers not only philosophical, but also ideological allegations. It implies that Natural law involves a notion that would never and could never be accepted in the positivist tradition: the subjective and therefore non-scientific notion of belief[66] as a criteria for legitimacy, represented by moral principles for acting, when not religious reasons for acting.

Therefore, for a Natural lawyer, the only definition of authority will be linked to the normative power emanating from a "superior" abstract and very general principle which will forcedly impose a determined value. Kelsen characterizes Natural Law Theory as the following:

> "If the 'nature' in which the norms of Natural Law are immanent is the nature of man, and if we consider that man's nature – unlike that of animals – consists in human reason, then Natural Law appears as the Law of Reason.

---

[65] Natural Law for Today's Lawyer (1957, p. 479).
[66] For a complete overview, cf. Reynolds, B. (1993).

> Since reason is the faculty of thought and knowledge, the norms of the Law of Reason present themselves as the meaning of acts of thought: they are not willed norms but thought norms. Now there is such a thing as a merely thought norm (as opposed to a positive norm posited by a real act of will); but it is not the meaning of an act of thought but rather of an act of will which does not occur in reality but is imagined or thought of in the same way as we can imagine or think of anything which is possible but does not exists in reality."[67]

Therefore, the main point is not even that the natural law doesn't fit the definitions traced by the positivist tradition, as anyone would expect, and by so falling out of the scope of what law is or is supposed to be according to legal positivism. The more basic point is rather that the natural law doesn't even step out of the descriptive field, where norms are simply thought because, instead of being produced by human will, they are only attained or reached by human reason, by an act of thinking.

What we actually observe here is a clear negation from the part of Kelsen of the notion of practical reason. Clearly, the normative field, the domain of the regulation of human behavior, cannot be ordered and ruled by particular statements derived from general abstract ideological metaphysical/theological formulas such as "do good and avoid evil", which are strange to the scientific aims of legal cognition itself.

---

[67] Kelsen, H. (1979, p.6).

4.2 Understanding the Tension

Considering the Kelsenian distinction between static and dynamic principles ruling the normative creation, the Natural law kind of normative systems were classified as ruled by a static principle (as moral orders), while the positivist normative systems are clearly ruled by a dynamic principle.

But then, since the Natural law norms seem to be inserted in a static normative system, where we take as point of departure a general widely-accepted abstract principle and derive every other norm from their content, there is no space left for the acts of will in the enactment of the derived norms. Therefore, these moral norms are not wanted norms, but merely thought norms, the result of a pure mental process of logical derivation. They are not the meaning of acts of human will, but are the result of rational deduction from the content of a general principle.

The positive legal system, on the contrary, is based on a dynamic principle which allows the agent to enact a valid legal norm, which is created as willed, more than merely thought. We have nothing to say about the "quality" of the content of such norms, but only about the legitimacy or not of their validity. It is the process of normative creation which is regulated by the norm itself, internally to the system at stake, which preserves also the kelsenian "principle of purity".

Many find in this approach an opportunity to criticize legal positivism as a fruitful field for totalitarian or anti-democratic regimes. However, Kelsen has never denied that a legal system indeed must be revised and criticized when in need. But the point is that such an activity is not the task of legal theory. It is only the legal science and its methodology which must be "purified", and it is the legal scientist who should isolate the legal norm from every "external" element, such as justice for example, in his study, analysis, explanation and interpretation of the legal norms. This methodological "separation" is very well illustrated in a passage coming from Kelsen's last, farewell lecture at the University of California in Berkeley on May 27th, 1952. The context is a by that time 71 years old Hans Kelsen, once forced himself to leave Germany during WWII:

> "And, indeed, I do not know, and I cannot say what justice is, the absolute justice for which mankind is longing. I must acquiesce in a relative justice and I can only say what justice is to me. Because science is my profession, and hence the most important thing in my life, justice, to me, is that social order under whose protection the search for truth can prosper. 'My' justice, then, is the justice of freedom, the justice of peace, the justice of democracy – the justice of tolerance."[68]

The fact of the lacking of objectivity for the concept of justice doesn't hinder the possibility for it to be an ideal to be searched for. The point is simply that this searching cannot be performed in a scientific frame. It is not possible, for example, to propose a strictly scientific theory that would ground some of the more basic Natural law principles such as *Lex injusta non est lex*, defended by St. Augustine and St. Thomas Aquinas, simply because the notion of justice is subjective. Then, even if we all can eventually agree with

---

[68] Kelsen, H. (2008 [1957], p. 24).

some general idea of justice, the real problems would arise later, when this general concept will be supposed to be applied in the many different cases...

In the context of positivism, the closest one can get to the notion of justice would be, in this sense, an almost formal notion of equity, meaning simply that similar cases must be treated similarly. But we must recognize that this formulation represents a very abstract, nearly empty or useless precept.

4.3 Overcoming the tension

Alf Ross gives a good overview of the tensions between legal positivism and natural law when he explains that:

> "This conflict is often treated as the most fundamental issue in legal philosophy, dividing the field into two hostile and irreconcilable camps. Positivists characterize natural law doctrines as beliefs based on metaphysical or religious ideas incompatible with the principles of scientific thought. Proponents of natural law theory, for their part, accuse their antagonists of failing to understand the realm of spirit and value, a realm that is real enough, although it cannot be discovered or described by means of sensory experience. Natural lawyers have even gone so far as to accuse the positivists of moral torpidity, and of complicity in the abominations of the Hitler regime."[69]

---

[69] Ross, A. (1961, p. 46).

As we understand, the critics coming from each of those fields and directed to each other are actually not based in an exact recognition of the methodological functions established by their corresponding legal theories. For that reason they seem to be somehow mixing the theory with the object to be studied. Let us see how that happens in more detail.

It is not that evident that the manner in which the Natural law jurists regard legal positivism is completely incompatible with their own view. Rather, it seems that, for a Natural law scientist, the positivist approach is merely "incomplete"[70], in the sense that it ignores the necessity of grounding for the basic precepts of a normative system in those most fundamental values that would also ground the life in society in a safe and constructive, rather than dangerous and destructive, "universal" intentions. Moreover, History has repeatedly taught us that, after a "high dose" of legal positivism, there were always the need to make reference to Natural law as the only means to re-establish the social order. Both systems seemed to have "interacted" in this sense. It is easy to recognize that aspect once we take for example the cases like the Nürnberg trials after World War II, where the war crimes committed were then qualified as crimes against humanity or as violations of the human rights.

At the same time, we believe that the positivist should not be blamed for the abnormal results that may come out of a positivist legal system, since also the natural lawyer is not safe from the possibility of the development of some abnormal possible beliefs that may be defended in the name of the Natural law system. Religious fanatical is one of the most frightening aspects

---

[70] But the relation is not transitive: for the positivist, the natural lawyer's approach is simply wrong.

of society. Nowadays, for example, the Brazilian federal congress is taken by numerous right-wing congressmen coming from military and/or religious background and defending clearly homophobic, racist statements and even expressly inciting hatred and violence against women and homosexuals. All of that is defended in the name of the interests and the preservation of the idea of the ideal "traditional Brazilian family". Those politicians are also the most voted ones during the Brazilian elections. So, this notion of idealized "common good" underlying such offensive and harmful claims, expressly mixing religious and personal beliefs in the interest of establishing laws corresponding to it, is it really humanistic? At the end of the day, what would be the ultimate criterion for defining the "natural" in Natural law?

4.4 Final Remarks on this Topic

The positivistic perspective will deny the legitimacy of natural law in the same way it denies morality as grounding for legal validity, because moral principles cannot be formally known, in the sense of being scientifically objectively defined.

But one thing that can be firmly stated is that, concerning the method for the description of the legal system, the frontiers between the two approaches are notably less marked. For the positivist scientist, or jurist, the task to be performed is the description of the fact of the existence of the norm, because the presence of a norm in a legal document is indeed a fact that can be attested, in the same way as the enaction of an individual norm in the frame of a trial, after it happens, it's also a fact that can be attested. Now, in the

General Theory of Norms, Kelsen proposes a legal theory not only for Law but also for Positive Morals, like the one based in Christianity.

Positive morals (the kind of system where we are able to recognize the creation and positing of every moral norm) it's actually a field where it's very difficult to establish the boundaries between positive and natural law. But what Kelsen is proposing is precisely a scientific theory about it, i.e., a rigid method capable of acknowledging the set of multiple moral norms as a material capable of rational cognition for a science like normative science. In this sense, it is important not to mix the theory of its object. But Kelsen is capable of offering a view of morality compatible with the positivistic approach, making it a fairly possible object of scientific knowledge:

> "Statements about the validity of moral norms are the sentences by which ethics (understood as a science) describes a certain morality, for instance the Judaeo-Christian morality posited by Moses and Jesus. In the mouth of God or of a person considered to be a prophet or the Son of God (i.e. a moral authority positing moral norms), the word *sollen* – say in the sentence 'You are not to kill' – has a prescriptive signification. For the sentence is a norm; it is the meaning of a divine act of will, mediated by the prophet or the Son of God, and directed to the behavior of human beings. In an ethics presenting – i.e. describing – Judaeo-Christian morality, the word *sollen* in the sentence 'A human being is not to kill other human beings' has a descriptive signification. The sentence of the ethicist is not a norm, for ethics as a science cannot prescribe anything, but only describe the norms given to it. As a scientist, the ethicist is no more competent to posit moral norms than the legal

> scientist is competent to posit legal norms; the ethicist has no more justification for claiming any moral authority than the legal scientist has for claiming any legal authority."[71]

With this approach, we are trying to show that, concerning at least some aspects, like the possibility of approach a moral normative system according to a positivist perspective, it is possible to render the limits between positivism and Natural law at least more flexible. Of course, there are limits to which this comparison might be pushed. But the positivism *qua* method of knowledge of a given set of norms is capable to report also norms involving non-scientific notions in their formulation, i.e., to attest their validity.

This empirical approach may be even more fitted to "softer" versions of legal positivism, such as the one proposed by Herbert Hart. The following passage illustrates why:

> *"The question whether a rule of recognition exists and what its content is, i.e. what the criteria of validity in any given legal system are, is regarded throughout this book as an empirical, though complex, question of fact."*[72]

The problem returns, of course, when those non-scientific notions are no longer simply a part of the content of the norm, but are also supposed to justify a set of norms as legally binding. This perspective, defended by the

---

[71] Kelsen, H. (1979, p.154-155).
[72] Hart, H. (1961, p.245).

Natural lawyers, cannot be taken seriously according to positivism, due to the lacking of objectiveness.

So, after this complex context, we seem to be forced to admit that, once in the frame of a theory aiming the objective grounding and the formal justification of a normative system, the reason for the validity of a norm, its formal legitimating, cannot make reference to something simply attested in its content, neither to an ultimate subjective element incapable of being scientifically approached. Rather than that, the reason that makes the norm binding has to relate to the authorization of the person enacting it, it has to be about the correctness of this process of creation. Similarly, the searching for the legitimating will go upwards the normative chain, until achieving the basic norm, which, in the case of positivism, is to be presupposed as a fiction. But the fact of being considered as a fiction doesn't mean that the basic norm is simply the meaning of an act of thought, as the moral norms according to the Natural law approach. In order to avoid that, Kelsen will defend the idea that the basic norm is the meaning of a non-real act of will, a fictive act of will. We will approach that problematic question further on our study.[73]

---

[73] Cf. chapter 6.

Chapter 5

Science and Method: the Naturalistic Fallacy

"Science is what we know and philosophy is what we don't know."
(Bertrand Russell, 1959)

As we have already seen, the legal theory of Hans Kelsen is marked by a strong interest in drawing a formal frame of analysis for normative systems. According to this author, the positive normative systems of Law and Morals must be neatly separated from the sciences describing them, i. e., from the legal science in the case of positive law and from the Ethics in the case of positive moral norms. In the same way, these normative sciences must themselves be separated from the natural sciences – such as Physics, for example –, inasmuch as the object of a legal science does not consist in facts expressed by sentences, but instead in valid norms which are expressed in the form of imperatives or prescriptions.

In this context, Kelsen claims that a common mistake consists in mixing those two separate domains, the "Is" domain of the facts and the "Ought" domain of the norms, what could give place to a series of problems in the field of legal theory and legal argumentation, such as the many quarrels involving the application of logical principles to norms (Jørgensen's Dilemma being the most notable example). This misunderstanding is known as "Naturalistic Fallacy", as pointed out by G. E. Moore in 1903' *Principia Ethica*.

The aim of this chapter will be to explain how Kelsen's theory relates this fallacy with the "Principle of Purity", and how it is possible to better understand and even aim to solve some classical legal problems derived from the involuntary falling into the Naturalistic Fallacy.

5.1 David Hume as a model

Michael Hartney, the translator of the *General Theory of Norms* from the original German to the English language tells that, in a personal conversation with Herbert Hart, the last has confirmed the fact that Kelsen used to say that *"Hume was the greatest philosopher of all times"*[74]. This is a very interesting remark that helps enlightening some of the perspectives Kelsen later assumes, namely regarding the aims in establishing "solid foundations" for his scientific theory, as well as the anti-metaphysical approach and the refutation of the notion of practical reason, together with the general interest in establishing a scrupulous methodological approach to science.

The most famous quotation regarding this methodological mistake (that was later called the *Naturalistic Fallacy* by G. E. Moore) is found in David Hume's *Treatise of Human Nature*, first published at the end of 1738. Hume says:

> "In every system of morality, which I have hitherto met with, I have always remarked that the author proceeds for some time in the ordinary way of reasoning, and establishes the

---

[74] Also confirmed by Otto, W. (1987, p.539).

> being of a God, or makes observations concerning human affairs; when of a sudden I am surprised to find, that instead of the usual copulations of propositions, *is*, and *is not*, I met with no proposition that is not connected with an *ought*, or an *ought not*. This change is imperceptible; but is, however, of the last consequence."[75]

After Hume and Moore, the problems and consequences behind the falling into the naturalistic fallacy were also expressed by the French mathematician and philosopher of science Henri Poincaré (1854 – 1912), who also denies the possibility of scientifically qualifying ethics, as he explains:

> "Now, the principles of science and the postulates of geometry are in the indicative mood and cannot be otherwise. This is also the mood of experimental truths; and all the sciences are founded on nothing but the indicative mood and cannot be founded in anything else. Thus, the most subtle dialectician can juggle these principles as he wills, combine them, pile them one on the top of the other: everything he will get from them will being the indicative mood. He will never get a sentence which says 'Do this' or 'Do not do that', i.e. a sentence which confirms or contradicts morality."[76]

---

[75] Hume, D. (2007 [1738], p.244/245).
[76] Poincaré, H. (1982/1913, p. 225).

More recently, this idea was also developed in detail by the English philosopher Richard Hare (1919 – 2002), whose approach is based on the notions of frastic and neustic in an attempt to deal with the problematic notion of practical syllogism, considered the most notable example of the use of the naturalistic fallacy.

But also Kelsen expressly makes reference to the "Hume Law" in order to corroborate one of the most basic postulates concerning his theory of legal positivism: that an Ought, a norm, cannot be derived from an Is, a causal rule or a description of a norm, as those present in legal science. Thus, to speak about the naturalistic fallacy in the context of Kelsen's positivist theory means a recall to be aware of the differences between what is stated in the real actual domain of our behavior and the evaluation of this behavior (good, bad, just and, regarding the scientific level, the evaluation of true/false descriptions about the norms) and, on the other hand, what is prescribed in the domain of Law itself. In the legal domain, the Ought which characterizes and defines a legal norm cannot be related to those subjective evaluations, but, instead, it's objectively determined by the notion of legal validity, which means, as we have already seen, the specific existence of the norm in a determined legal or moral positive system.

Therefore, in order to understand the presence of the fallacy in the field of the positive legal theory, one must understand the existence of this fundamental gap between what belongs to the factual scope of events and what belongs to the normative scope of norms regulating those events. In this first attempt to draw the limits between the causal domain of the human acts ordered by the laws of causality and the legal domain ordered by the laws of normative imputation, it would be useful to analyze some examples of ordinary acts of the daily life which may however receive a special legal interpretation. About this issue, it is Kelsen himself who gives us several examples of a variety of ordinary acts which can be differently interpreted according to the Law:

> "For example: People assemble in a large room, make speeches, some raise their hands, others do not – this is the external happening. Its meaning is that a statute is being passed, that law is created… To give other illustrations: A man in a robe and speaking from a dais says some words to a man standing before him, legally this external happening means: a juridical decision was passed. A merchant writes a letter of a certain content to another merchant who, in turn, answers with a letter; this means they have concluded a legally binding contract. Somebody causes the death of somebody else; legally, this means a murder."[77]

To Kelsen, norms are still essentially linked to human actions that are having place in the factual field of our everyday life. Deryck Beyleveld andRoger Brownsword wisely synthesize that *"To interpret an act in terms of its legal meaning is to view the act in relation to a norm that is viewed as a legally valid norm"*[78]. But, in order to better understand this relation, we must analyze more closely this concept of "ought".

5.1.1 *The "Ought"*

---

[77] Kelsen, H. (1960, p.2).
[78] Beyleveld, D.&Brownsword, R. (1998, p. 116).

As we have mentioned before, norms can be taken in consideration when a certain act is being specifically interpreted: not causally interpreted, but normatively interpreted. This allows us to say that a norm represents some kind of mechanism of interpretation. More precisely, according to Kelsen, norms are meanings; they are the objective meaning of a subjective act. However, the act in question is also somehow restricted: the norm is the meaning of an act of will from a person, directed to another person's behavior.

Of course one could argue that all those acts listed in the example abovementioned could also be interpreted in other different ways, if one would have wanted to do so. The point is, precisely, that the law gives to those acts a *specific* interpretation, according to a previous valid norm existent in a determined system with a corresponding content. Therefore, it is the norm already belonging to the legal system which gives us the key for interpreting the specific legal or normative meaning of those arbitrary acts taking place in the causal realm of our everyday life. Departing from this frame, a new particular norm can then be created, regarding the very case in question. Thus, this "new" norm will be dependent of two main elements: the existence of a previous positive valid norm, and an act of will in regard to which this new norm will be the objective meaning.

Concerning the "objectiveness" in question, Deryck Beyleveld and Roger Brownsword make this prudent observation:

> "As we understand Kelsen, he is not saying (…) that a norm is objectively valid (that an 'ought' has an objective meaning) on condition that everyone agrees that the behavior prescribed ought to be done. It is not a consensus of wills that converts a subjective 'ought' into an objective 'ought'.

> He is saying that to regard a norm as being objectively valid is (that is, means) to regard what the norm prescribes as binding upon all whose behavior (actual or potential) is being addressed by the norm regardless of whether anyone (including the person who is doing this objective regarding) wishes this behavior or not (that is, regardless of whether anyone wills this 'ought' in the subjective sense)."[79]

So, the definition of "norm" is indeed linked to the concept of a command or an order, but with the important detail that this order must come from an authorized person, as an expression – mostly in the form of an imperative – of a will. Since this will must come from a person authorized by the Law itself, there is always a strict relation between the legal production and the legal power. According to Norberto Bobbio[80], to enact a norm is always to be able to do so, and the authorization comes from no one but the Law itself. This shows the importance of the fact that the methodological procedures to manage the relations between the legal norms and handle the variety of possible legal affairs must always come from the Law itself, something that also illustrates the constant concern to preserve the principle of "purity".

So, to sum up, what is needed to create a positive legal norm? First of all, there must be a prior, more general norm to support the existence of the new one. Then, the "creative" subject must be an authorized person capable of enacting an objective act of will. Those are the elements necessary to characterize the norm as a valid one: its specific existence in the frame of a legal order; the fact of its connection to a legal system via a more general

---

[79] Beyleveld & Brownsword (1998, p. 118).
[80] Bobbio, N. (2008).

norm, and the compulsoriness that links up all its addressees. This late obligatory aspect is in fact the objectiveness aspect involving the act of will coming from the Judge or the Legislator. An act of will with a subjective meaning consists only in a command, without legal force, it means the expression of a personal will towards a specific case, and doesn't even enters the normative legal level. Instead, the act of will with an objective meaning has to come only from an authorized, impartial, neutral person, and it's precisely the meaning of this objective act of will that represent a legal norm.

In this perspective, we can sustain that, while the command is the expression of a desire, the norm is the expression of a duty, of an "ought" (*Sollen*). The notion of "Ought" introduces us to the separation between the legal prescriptive field of the norms – the domain of the "Ought" – and the factual descriptive field of the legal science – the domain of the "is". This distinction addresses us again to the main problem we intend to analyze here: the Naturalistic Fallacy.

5.1.2 *The "Is"*

Now, in Kelsen's theory, it is very clear that the principle of "purity" guiding the work of the jurist is directly linked with the problem of the naturalistic fallacy. The fact that a norm can only be created via the existence of a previous norm, or, said in another words, that an 'ought' can only be created once given the existence of a previous 'ought', states the necessity of staying in one and the same scope, namely, the normative, legal one. The "purity" here also indicates that it is necessary to stay inside this normative level in order to *create* new norms, and that the "ought" characterizing the norm must not be mixed with the factual elements pertaining to the domain of the "Is". Practically speaking, this means that the norm must not be confounded with the external elements which may be inserted in this legal level. One consequence would be the impressive remark that norms don't need to express a just content in order to be accepted as valid norms. Fairness or justice are outer elements depending on subjective moral principles, and stay completely strange to the "pure" field of legal positivism. The same might happen with psychological, sociological and political aspects involving norms. Kelsen argues that the admission of such elements will lead to a fallacy, that one must not deduce that something *might be* the case simply because something *is* the case. Similarly, one cannot establish that something might be the case simply based on the fact that something is (subjectively) *believed* to be the case. One field is regulated by reasoning processes, the other by intentional acts of will.

So, the naturalistic fallacy appears in Kelsen's theory when is question of separating the normative field from the indicative one. In a practical perspective, this is represented by the division or the gap which needs to exist between the system composed by norms on one side, and the legal science describing those norms on the other.

We must note that the great distinction between the legal norm and the sentences of the legal theory (or legal science) lies in the fact that the sentence can, among other qualifications, also be qualified according to truth values, while the norm can only be said to be valid. Actually, even the facts themselves linguistically expressed in the sentences cannot be valued as true or false, but only as existing or not existing: true or false are only the descriptions made about the existence of those facts. The predicates true/false can be said only in relation to elements of the "is" domain, to the descriptions of the facts which can be made by any science. But they are not linked to the very object of these sciences, as the natural facts, for instance. On the other side, the norm is exactly the object being described by the legal science, and it can, equally, only be said to be existent or not existent. The point is that when the norm is said to be existent, this means that it is a valid norm (here "valid norm" is actually a pleonasm), and the very existence of the norm in the legal system constitutes already its validity. The validity of a norm is therefore simply and nothing more than its specific existence.

5.2 One Example of the Fallacy: Jørgensen's Dilemma

According to the traditional conceptions of logic entailment, which Kelsen searches in the traditional notion of Aristotelian syllogism, the conclusion will follows from the two premises if and only if the conclusion cannot be false if the premises are true. This is the "rule of inference" Kelsen analyses when dealing with the question whether norms can be created via a similar form. In the case of the syllogism, the inference is logically valid or not depending on the evaluation of the sentences according to the values of true and false. The problem arises when imperatives, commands, legal or moral norms are inserted in this kind of syllogism. This happens in the so-called practical syllogisms, where a norm is supposed to be "created" from a general norm, together with the fact attesting its content. But, clearly, since norms cannot be evaluated according to truth values, they cannot play the role of premises and/or conclusion, because there's no way to evaluate the validity of a norm only by means of logical reasoning.

All of that appears to be straightforward. Nevertheless, when we first start looking to some of the examples of these so-called practical syllogisms, the conclusion seems to follow as inescapably as in a valid legal argument expressed by a theoretical syllogism. Let us take the example:

> Love your neighbors.
> John is your neighbor.
> ―――――――――――――
> Love John.

It seems impossible to argue against the validity of such an argument. This difficulty was first expressed by Jørgen Jørgensen in 1937, and was named the "Jørgensen's Dilemma" by Alf Ross, in 1941. Jørgensen explains himself:

> "So we have the following puzzle: According to a generally accepted definition of logical inference only sentences which are capable of being true or false can function as premises or conclusions in an inference; nevertheless it seems evident that a conclusion in the imperative mood may be drawn from two premises one of which or both of which are in the imperative mood."[81]

As we've seen, according to Kelsen, there is a "methodological abyss", a gap between the "Ought" (*Sollen*) domain, tenanted by norms; and the "Is" (*Sein*) domain, tenanted by sentences. Jørgensen's dilemma puts in question which kinds of interaction seem to prevail in the relation between prescriptions or imperatives (*Sollsätze*) and descriptions or sentences (*Sätze*).

But, when considering the differences between the norms and description of norms, Kelsen keeps insisting that the two cannot be reducible or even

---

[81] Jørgensen, J. (1937, p.290).

comparable. One is the Law, and the other is the science that describes the Law as its object. Kelsen says:

> "'Is' and 'Ought' are purely formal concepts, two forms or modes which can assume any content whatsoever, but which must assume some content in order to be significant. It is something which is, and it is something which ought to be. But no specific content follows from the form."[82]

In order to explain the relation between form and content regarding the legal norm and the legal proposition of the science, Kelsen introduces the notion of *modally indifferent substrate*[83]. So, if we consider the following sentences:

1. "Al Capone ought to pay the taxes." and

2. "Al Capone pays/had paid his taxes."

we have one modally indifferent substrate, which is the behavior "paying the taxes", which happens to be under two different modes, namely, once under the "ought" form in 1. And after under the "is" form in 2. Their content is identical, but the linguistic formulations themselves are not comparable, correspondent or deductible one from another.

So, concerning Jørgensen's dilemma, if we stick to Kelsen's conception of the modally indifferent substrate, we must notice that, in fact, the modally indifferent substrate is neither true nor false in itself. It can only be the content of a true/false sentence, in the same way that it can only be the

---

[82] Kelsen, H. (1979, p.60).
[83] The notion of modally indifferent substrate and its relation to Jørgensen's dilemma will be the main topic of the chapters 8 and 9.

content of a valid norm. But there is no intrinsic correspondence between a true/false sentence and a valid norm; they only happen to have a similar modally indifferent substrate.

So, when Jørgensen says that the answer to the dilemma is only a matter of translation (true indicative sentences could be identified and "translated" into valid norms or imperatives), actually there is absolutely no correspondence between an imperative or a norm and an indicative sentence: the fact is that we are simply dealing with a modally indifferent substrate, which is presented or "dressed up" in two different modes. To sum up, the point of interest is that Kelsen's notion of the modally indifferent substrate is outside the bounds of any bivalent logical approach.

To Kelsen, every norm must have content, the "modally indifferent substrate", which is not the indicative factor, as Jørgensen's believed the content of the imperative to be, but rather the very behavior wanted by the *imperator*. So, in one way, the person enacting the norm knows the content of the norm that will be enacted, his will will be concerning some specific behavior, that will be expressed or indicated by the norm to be created. This act of thought concerning the norm is somehow the "first" step preceding the act of will of the agent. And on the other way, also the addressee of the norm must likewise understand what is he supposed to do, how is he supposed to behave, and he does that by observing what is the content of the norm. Let's see how this relation is manifested in an example. Consider the following situation:

"Every citizen should pay the taxes" consist in a valid norm, let us say. This norm also applies to, for example, the citizen Al Capone. Once a year this individual receives a letter saying how much he has to pay to the government, as income taxes. The legal norm behind the letter, putted in a simpler way, says that "Every citizen must pay his/her taxes", even if this very prescriptive element is not explicitly formulated in the text addressed to Al Capone. It is somehow implicit on the fact of having the bill addressed to him. The norm-positing subject can nevertheless justify his demanding for the money, if needed, by enumerating the benefits to be seized by the citizens, like the improvement of social and public services, the reduction of budget deficits (though he doesn't need to, given his authorization). In Kelsen's theory, those aspects related to having a norm posed to one's behavior and immediately knowing how to proceed are to be seen as acts of thinking regarding the norm, and they have nothing to do with the willing positing the norm as valid and binding. They have nothing to do with the modally indifferent substrate, which is, in this case, the neutrals "to pay the taxes" or "paying the taxes". Those neutrals are the content of the norm. Thus, by receiving the letter and checking the sum to be paid, Al Capone *knows* the implicatures of is adhering or ignoring the bill. He *knows* everything that's "behind" the bill, by "dressing" the normative content in a descriptive "outfit", by means of his acts of thought.

So, what happens when we are confronted with the notion of practical syllogism is that we are confounding our act of thought about the content of the norm and the act of will providing the norms' validity. The general problem of the relation between imperatives and statements is much simpler when we only take into consideration the legal field (apart from all the other imperatives or "ordinary" orders). Then we can argue that, even if we somehow know the content of the norm which is "supposed to be created" by the Judge in a simple case, it's only the enaction of the individual norm by the Judge that will render the imperative a legitimate valid legal norm.

The misleading "practical syllogism" actually works in our daily lives because we are in fact simply reasoning about the norms involved in the inference, through acts of thought. The fallacy emerges when we try to trespass this level and admit that we are actually creating a valid norm from the existence of a true sentence plus the fact of the existence of a previous norm. It is, indeed, natural that we try to understand what the norm is demanding, in order to know how to behave. The minor premise which poses a fact is actually the context in which we legitimate are reasoning by acts of thought, and the major premise (indicating a norm in the practical syllogism) poses the norm that we must understand, comprehend, which presents the behavior wanted as its content. If I understand the first premise in the context of the second premise, I'm able to know which behavior I'm supposed to have, I can tell what the modally indifferent substrate is. All this procedure does not touch the normative level, because no objective act of will has yet being considered or enacted. It's all a question of knowing what is at stake, i.e. of considering the given facts through mental processes.

Moreover, we must also notice that, as the *imperator*, it is perfectly possible to understand the content of a general norm, together with the corresponding fact and still do not want to posit the individual behavior as obligatory in the conclusion. The particular norm posed as a conclusion in the practical syllogism will only be a valid binding norm after the adding of an objective act of will. Until that moment, we remain in the realm of the Is, where no valid legal norm might be created.

5.3 **Final remarks on this topic**

The legacy of the naturalistic fallacy is relevant to make the important remark that norms cannot be the result of conclusions of our reason or, said in another manner, of rational deduction. David Hume states that:

> "Reason is the discovery of truth or falsehood. Truth or falsehood consists in an agreement or disagreement either to the real relations of ideas, or to real existence and matter of fact. Whatever, therefore, is not susceptible of this agreement or disagreement, is incapable of being true or false, and can never be an object or our reason"[84].

As we have seen, Jørgensen's dilemma is a perfect example of the application of this misleading procedure.

However, Kelsen's theory represents a fine example of the application of David Hume's recommendations warning us to the mistakes derived from this mixing of the two different levels, Is and Ought. In the frame of our study, this represents an appeal from legal theory to the methodological principles coming from the philosophical domain. The interesting detail to notice is that the notion of naturalistic fallacy displays, in a perfect manner, Kelsen's concerns about the correct treatment of the normative field as the object of the scientific approach.

The positive outcome of the avoiding of the naturalistic fallacy is the widening of the perspective about the legitimate approach of norms and the process of normative creation. In this sense, by respecting the boundaries of prescriptive and descriptive fields, one can clearly understand that it is perfectly acceptable to make inferences about the fact of the existence of a

---

[84] Hume, D. (2007 [1738], p. 240).

norm, in order, for example, to justify the legitimating of the normative creation once it has already happened. This is allowed by the important notion of modally indifferent substrate, which we briefly introduced in this chapter, but that will be further treated in another part of the present study.[85] By attempting to the fallacy, we can fully grasp the idea that norms have form and content in the same manner as the descriptions about their validity, but then we must also recognize that, nevertheless, this aspect does not allow the possibility of deriving norms from facts or descriptions, nor to establish direct logical relations between them.

The fact that norms are supposed to be left in this "pure" prescriptive level does not attest that they are unreachable or inaccessible to human discourse, evaluation or study. It only attests that those aspects, even if fundamental for the juridical scientific approach, are still irrelevant for the creation and application of legal norms.

---

[85] Cf. chapters 8 and 9.

Chapter 6

The Non-Existence in Legal Science

> *"It's no wonder that truth is stranger than fiction.*
> *Fiction has to make sense."*
> Mark Twain

If the presence of fiction in natural sciences is sufficiently known and accepted, the same doesn't seem to be the case when it comes to its legitimacy in legal science, as we will see in the present chapter.

The presence of fictions as a part of the legal system, within the formulation of the norms, can actually be traced since Roman law, even if its legitimacy also in that level remains a matter of great divergence among critics. Nevertheless, the legitimacy of the use of fictions by natural sciences or philosophy is attested by famous examples of thought experiments, for instance. It is sufficient to think, for example, about Schrödinger's cat or the twin paradox (or Langevin paradox) in physics, as well as the twin Earth thought experiment in philosophy. They function as a scientific tool allowing to more easily explain and understand the concepts or theses they are referring to.

Considering this context, in this chapter we will analyze the use of fictions made by this special kind of science dealing with the regulation of our behavior, namely legal science. The fundamental question to be approached is whether the basic norm, to be presented as a fiction, has a normative or prescriptive profile.

Our aim is to analyze the use of fiction by the legal science under the light of the legal theory proposed by Kelsen, especially concerning his proposal that the legitimization of the whole positive legal system is based on a fiction, called the Basic Norm (*Grundnorm*). The thesis we sustain is that this "norm" must be seen as a purely methodological or scientific tool (just like the thought experiments of physics and philosophy), and not as an ordinary legal norm among others in the positive normative system. We will try to elucidate how can a fiction display such an important scientific function and still preserve the "principle of purity" of the Kelsenian legal theory.

6.1 Legal science: Meaning and Particularities

As we have already many times insisted in express, it is a central aspect of the kelsenian legal philosophy the fact that the Law, namely the overall set of norms, must be clearly separated from the science that describes and studies this normative set. Another differentiation cherished by Kelsen separates neatly this kind of normative science, which takes the legal or moral norm as its object, from the natural sciences, which takes the facts of nature as its object. These two ideas constitute the methodological frame in which Kelsen formulates his *Pure Theory of Law*. It is also the notion of "purity" that allows one to deal with each one of these Kelsenian paradigms.

The fact of confusing Law and Legal Science was a common mistake made by some of Kelsen's contemporaries[86]. Certainly, one should concede that the content of legal science, in the context of legal Positivism, can indeed sometimes be very confusing. The theory of Law describes the norms of a particular normative system[87], but the point is that the norm described by the science has no longer its normative power or, in the terms of Kelsen, it is no longer a valid norm. It is exactly the fact of the validity of the norm that is being described, and a fact cannot (legally) compel anyone.

But let us start from the beginning, by recalling some aspects concerning the term "legal norm" according to Kelsen's positivist theory.

The definition of "norm" is relied to the concept of a command or an order, with the important detail that this order must come from an authorized person, as an expression – mostly in the form of an imperative – of a will. Since this *will* must come from a person authorized by the Law itself, there is always a strict relation between the legal production and the legal power[88]. The norm is the meaning of an objective act of will, coming from an authorized person. It is marked by the presence of the "ought" particle[89], meaning that we're not in the domain of the "Is", but in the domain of the "Ought" (*Sollen*). Kelsen says:

> "When someone commands or prescribes, he wills that something ought to happen. The Ought – the norm – is the meaning of a willing or act of will, and – if the norm is a

---

[86] This "confusion" is linked to the denial of the duality of "Is" and "Ought". In order to see how Kelsen treats and analyses several classical cases, Cf. KELSEN, H (1979, p. 63-82).
[87] Cf. Spaak, T. (2005, p. 397- 414).
[88] Cf. van Roermund, B. (2000, p. 201-222).
[89] Even if the norm in question is not mandatory, but concerning permissions, empowerment or derogation, the "ought" element is always preserved.

prescription or command – it is the meaning of an act directed to the behavior of another person, an act whose meaning is that another person (or persons) is to behave in a certain way".[90]

According to Bobbio[91], to enact a norm is always to be able to do so, and the authorization comes from no one but the Law itself. This shows the importance of the fact that the procedures to manage the legal norms and handle the legal affairs must always come from the Law itself, according also to the principle of "purity"[92].

6.1.1 *Some examples*

So, again, what is needed to create a positive legal norm? First of all, legal validity is linked to the specific existence of a norm; second, to the fact of its belonging to a legal system; and third, to the compulsoriness that links up all its addressees. Those three elements are nevertheless related in an intrinsic manner. In our context, this late obligatory aspect is very important, and it is in fact the objectiveness of the meaning given to the act of will coming from the Judge/Legislator. A *subjective* meaning of the act of will consists in a command without legal force, it means the expression of a personal will

---

[90] Kelsen, H. (1979, p.2).
[91] Bobbio, N. (1997).
[92] What is implicit in this conception is that there is no place to logical treatment in the inner domain of Law, i. e. in the production or interpretation (decision) of legal norms.

towards a specific case, and that's not what Law is about. The *objective* meaning of the act of will comes only from an authorized, impartial, neutral person, and this objective meaning of this act of will is what ultimately defines the legal norm[93].

Now let us think of one example. Consider a "community" of pirates, for instance. Their community is hierarchically organized, with solid efficiently rules of behavior, which are enforced by the systematized application of sanctions. They seem to experience a very solid and efficient legal order! Nevertheless, regarding this example, Kelsen would certainly point out the lacking of objectiveness concerning the meaning of the act of will regarding the pirates. In the regress for searching the justification of those norms, there is no grounding for the enaction of the multiple norms composing their normative order, which might be rather seen as an (organized) agglomerate of orders[94].

While the command or the order is the expression of an arbitrary desire, the valid norm is the expression of a duty, of an obligatory action, of an "ought" (*Sollen*). The binding element is present only in this last *Sollen* form of command. The notion of "ought" introduces us one more time to the separation between the legal prescriptive field of the norms – the domain of

---

[93] By this approach, an objective command is not only the psychic event of the expression of a will. This can be seen in the case of a testament, for instance. In a valid testament, the subjective act of will of the person in question obtains its objectivity trough the Law: once it is legally legitimated, the command of the person in question will remain beyond his own existence, when he will no longer be able to express his will. This demonstrates the independency of the compulsoriness of the command from the subjective act of will.

[94] Actually, what turns a legal norm into a binding norm is the fact of assuming the existence of the Basic Norm in relation to such a normative system. We come to this issue later in this text.

the "ought" – and the factual descriptive field of sentences composing the legal science – the domain of the "is".

Concerning the relations between the science and its scientific object – here, legal science and Law itself – the English legal philosopher Herbert Hart[95] uses a great example to illustrate the fact that, even if the legal science deals with valid norms, it doesn't have any normative legal power[96]. He uses the example of the relation between someone who speaks a foreign language and his, let's say, English interpreter. If a German captain in a concentration camp says out loud to his English or American prisoners *"Stehen Sie auf!"*, the interpreter will probably also say out loud the words "Stand up!". The interpreter will do his best to show, by his intonation maybe, or by the expression in his face, that what the Captain said was not a begging or a simple request: it was an order. The point is: how do we must consider the sentence "Stand up!" in respect of its original in German? Is it a second order? Is it the same order? Is it the emission of an order? Well, the interpreter has no authority to emit orders. His job is to interpreter the orders of the captain and, if the order is obeyed or not, it was the Captain who was therefore obeyed or disobeyed. Hart then says that, in perfect accordance to Kelsen's theory, what happens in such a case is that the captain's order is being described by the interpreter, that the "Stand up!" was an order in a descriptive sense, that the original imperative was used in a descriptive, not prescriptive, sense.

While the example of the pirates show the absolute necessity of a fundament that gives the unity of a legal system, allowing it to be rationally acknowledged and scientifically investigated, the example of the interpreter

---

[95] Hart, H. (2005 [1963]).
[96] This aspect is essential to our future analysis of the Basic Norm as an element of legal science, and not of Law itself.

displays the relations between those norms with what is produced by the legal scientist.

6.1.2 Dichotomies in Kelsen's Theory

As we already could see, the legal philosophy of Hans Kelsen is essentially marked by its manifold dichotomies. When questions about the purposes of the legal sciences are at stake, another dichotomy then arises: the legal science is a descriptive science inasmuch as it doesn't make any prescription; but, at the same time, the objects of its descriptions are not statements, but prescriptions. Consequently, the normative science makes descriptions about prescriptions. Norberto Bobbio finely analyzes this issue:

> "'Normative' is in opposition (already in the *Hauptprobleme*) not to 'descriptive', but to 'explicative'; and, in parallel, 'descriptive' is in opposition (especially in the last works) not to 'normative', but to 'prescriptive'. Given that the doubles 'normative-explicative' and 'prescriptive-descriptive' do not superimpose themselves, there is no contradiction in affirming, as Kelsen does, that the legal science is at the same time descriptive and normative: descriptive in the sense that it does not prescribe, normative in the sense that the things being described are not facts, but norms, i.e., it is descriptive not about what exists, but about what ought to be. As *Sollsätze*, the propositions which characterize the legal science are distinguished in one hand from the *Seinsätze*

belonging to social sciences (causal), and, on the other hand, from the *Sollnormen* of any normative system."[97]

What Bobbio tries to explain is that the normative science, despite the fact of dealing with norms – where the "normative" term comes from –, does not make use of a prescriptive discourse, that is, its descriptions don't have the aim of changing the behavior of others. They are placed in the domain of the "is".

6.2 The Basic Norm as a scientific fiction

After the preceding considerations, one should be tended to imagine what the legitimate object of a legal science really looks like. Kelsen sustains a hierarchical vision of the legal system (the object of the legal science), in the form of a triangle or a pyramid, where the base is formed by the particular norms created[98] by the Judge in the tribunals. Those norms must be based on the validity of more general norms, and that searching for grounding happens until we arrive at the Constitution of a Country, for example. Then, one could still regress and go up on the pyramid to attain the very first Constitution of a Country, historically speaking. This searching is performed

---

[97] Bobbio, N. (2008, p. 58). This quotation was a personal translation of a Portuguese version of this book.
[98] Maybe it would be more correctly said that the Judge doesn't create any norm, he only applies the norms present on the system. But it won't be entirely wrong to say that particular or individual norms are actually created by the Judge, since they ultimately result from his particular act of will.

by the legal science, in its analysis of the legal norm as an object capable of being rationally described as a part of science.

The legal positivism (contrarily to the "antagonist" schools of thought such as the legal realism or the Natural law tradition) focuses on the claim that the norm and the Law are human constructions – they must be posited, enacted by someone – and the central notion is not the efficacy of a norm, or the moral value of a norm, but its validity, its existence and legitimate belonging to the legal system. The scientific justification of the validity of a system, of its legitimate existence as such, is based on the validity of the multiple norms composing it.

6.2.1 *The Searching for Justification*

A special question that naturally arises in the scientific context of the justification of the normative system refers to what would make a unity from the multiple norms of a Country, for example. That is, how does the multiplicity of types of legal norms can be unified, composing one system. Well, the first response to that question would probably mention the Constitution. The particular norms applied by the Judge (by his particular acts of will) in the tribunals would be supported by the general norms created by the Legislator (by his particular acts of will), and that's how we arrive, at the end, at the Constitution. But here we have to face a problem: from where does the Constitution obtain its validity? From a prior Constitution, one could say. But from where does the first Constitution of a Country (that earlier here we have placed in the top of the normative "pyramid") obtain its own validity? Or, in other words, the person who enacted the first Constitution of a Country, the very first Legislator, was authorized by whom to perform such an activity? How did it get legal legitimacy?

Here's the difficulty: every time we'll put a prior legal document as posited in this regression, the question about its legitimacy will be at stake. To solve this problem, Kelsen will say that what gives the foundations of the legal system cannot be a positive norm, a written document, because this norm would forcedly again have to be supported by a previous norm, and the person enacting this norm would have to obtain the power to create it from anyone from a even higher degree of competence. So, Kelsen will say, what legitimizes the creation of the first Constitution of a Country or, more generally, what legitimizes and gives the unity to a whole legal system, is in fact not a positive, but a fictive norm, called the Basic Norm[99].

What we will advocate here is that this Basic Norm is not placed in the legal system, on the top of the pyramid, as many critics of Kelsen suggest. We will defend that the Basic Norm is nothing more than a scientific fiction, a methodological tool. But, more precisely, our original approach will suggest that the regression in the seeking for the legitimating of the system must actually stop at the Constitution, and what we actually need after arriving there is not a new element, but a scientific tool used to conveniently consider this last object according to the positivist claims. It's only when we arrive at the top of the pyramid that we finally need the notion of Basic Norm, in order to rationally consider the first Constitution of a Country as the elementary component of the legal order.

---

[99] If we were to (wrongly) give some formulation to the Basic Norm, for didactic purposes let's say, it would sound like "We should do as the first Constitution of this Country tells us to do".

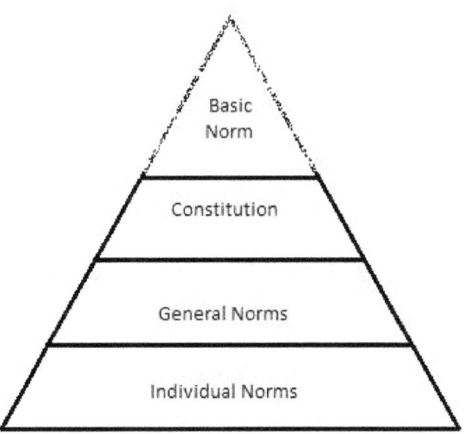

In fact, we believe that the legal system should be illustrated by an isosceles trapezoid instead of a triangle or pyramid.

The fact of clearly placing the Basic Norm in the scientific level will bring many clarifications to the kelsenian approach. First, the principle of purity will not be harmed by the presence of a fiction. Second, the theoretical aim of the Basic Norm will be preserved, since it's clear that the Basic Norm is not a norm to be respected by the individuals – it is not an effective norm. Lastly, the only problem that could remain, and also the more difficult one, will be related to questions of the form: "But why do Kelsen call the Basic Norm a *norm*?".

Our answer to this question makes reference to the fact that the fictive character of the Basic Norm concerns precisely its validity (and, as far as we remember, "validity" equals to "specific existence of a norm"), so it is the validity of this "norm" that makes reference a fiction. But what is fictional about the Basic Norm?

6.2.2 Understanding the Fiction

There is a difference between the fiction of the Basic Norm and the usual fictions present in Law among the other norms of the legal system[100]. The most common types of legal fiction will include contradictory elements expressly in the normative formulation, leading to an apparently impossible situation, with the objective of attaining a specific goal. Let's see some examples:

> "In property law, a husband and wife could be treated as one person. In family law, a child's will is attributed to his guardian. In the interpretation of wills, one spouse may be deemed to have predeceased the other, even though that may not in fact have been the case. Under the attractive nuisance doctrine, a child who trespasses is treated as having been invited onto the defendant's land. In immigration law, an alien may be considered to be legally excluded from the United States even though he is physically within its borders. In civil forfeiture proceedings, property itself may be named as a party to litigation (...)."[101]

Clearly, the Basic Norm doesn't share the same characteristics of the so-called legal fictions, that is to say the norms including contradictory elements

---

[100] For the relations between fictions and the normative level, Cf. Sievers, J. & Rahman, S. (2011).

[101] Student Author (2002, p. 2233-2234).

in their formulation. So, where is the fiction concerning the Basic Norm? How can we recognize it as a fiction?

6.2.3 A Little Help of Philosophy: Vaihinger's "As-If" approach

To elaborate the notion of Basic Norm as a fiction (a conception which is present only in the last writings of Kelsen – before the Basic Norm was seen as an hypothesis[102]), Kelsen searches for the foundations of his conception of fiction in the work "*The Philosophy of As-If*"[103], by the German philosopher Hans Vaihinger (1852-1933). To Kelsen, the fictional element concerns the *act* of conceiving the foundations for the legal system: we make "as if" there were a higher norm above the first Constitution, in order to stop the searching for legitimacy and to give to the system a unity.

So, in the case of the Basic Norm, the fictive element cannot be placed in the formulation of the norm. To formulate the Basic Norm expressly in the legal system means to submit it to a higher justification, is to presuppose that there is a higher power above it, in order to legitimize its creation. So, it is not the case that its formulation will give rise to contradictions but, more fundamental than that, the very fact of being formulated will already abort its specific function. Once formulated, the Basic Norm is legally enacted and enters in the circular searching for its own legitimacy. Kelsen himself explains

---

[102] In his previous writings (Kelsen, H. 1960), Kelsen tended to see the Basic Norm not as a fiction, but as a hypothesis. This approach was abandoned because Kelsen got aware from the fact that the "existence" of the Basic Norm would never be able to be verified. Contrary to hypotheses which are constructed with the very aim to be lately confirmed or falsified, the Basic Norm is presupposed with the consciousness of its impossibility of ever being verified.
[103] Vaihinger, H. (1965 [1911]).

this difference, showing that the fact of accepting the necessity of a fictive Basic Norm does not imply accepting the presence of fictions in Law:

> "According to Vaihinger, a fiction is a cognitive device used when one is unable to attain one's cognitive goal with the material at hand (1935:13). The cognitive goal of the Basic Norm is to ground the validity of the norms forming a positive moral or legal order, that is, to interpret the subjective meaning of the norm-positing acts as their objective meaning (i.e. as valid norms) and to interpret the relevant acts as norm-positing acts. This goal can be attained only by means of a fiction. It should be noted that the Basic Norm is not a hypothesis in the sense of Vaihinger's philosophy of As-If – as I myself have sometimes characterized it – but a fiction. A fiction differs from a hypothesis in that it is accompanied – or ought to be accompanied – by the awareness that reality does not agree with it." [104]

6.3 Where is the Basic Norm?

If we cannot formulate the Basic Norm in the terms of a prescription, it clearly means that it is not a regular norm, a valid norm or an efficient norm. We cannot obey or disrespect the Basic Norm. Its purpose is not that of

---

[104] Kelsen, H. (1979, p.256).

controlling our behavior. That is precisely the key to understand the notion of Basic Norm in Kelsen's theory. We sustain that the searching for the justification stops at the First Constitution: whatever comes after concerns no longer the Law, but only the legal science. By that perspective, the Basic Norm has no interest to the lawyer or the judge, neither to the defendant or the complainant. It is a matter of scientific understanding of the system, in the terms that the legal system could not be rationally described without the notion of the Basic Norm. The Basic Norm appears in the act of the jurist when he is confronted to the problem of the formal justification of the whole system of legal norms. The jurist need to presuppose the existence of a fiction of the Basic Norm, otherwise the legal system would be nothing but a chaotic heap of norms.

Our point is to clear up the fact that the Basic Norm finds its fictive element in the act of doing "as if" it existed. To conceive the Basic Norm consists in an act that involves the presumption of its existence, even though we know that the Basic Norm cannot exist. The fictiveness of this "norm" opposes anyone to identify it in any level: the Basic Norm is not a positive norm, but neither a formulated principle found in legal science. The point is that nobody is able to formulate, to construct or linguistically express such a thing as the Basic Norm. If it is enacted, we enter in the vicious circle and we need a new element to justify its existence as a norm. If it is formulated as a scientifically principle, it loses its purpose, which is to end the regression for justification and serve as the base for the legal system. What we defend is that the key to understand the needing of a Basic Norm is to see it as *a part of the process* of justifying the system, as a scientific *attitude* in front of the legal structure. To put it in another way: we only can understand the legal system as a rational ensemble of norms from the moment when we presuppose the fiction of a Basic Norm as being the starting point of the normative creation. The presupposition of the Basic norm is the condition *sine qua non* for the legal system to be a valid one (as a whole).

That's why do we have to call the Basic Norm a norm. The fiction about the Basic Norm is found precisely in its validity. We have to make "as if" there was a Basic Norm, because we know that it cannot be valid, it cannot legally exist. But we make "as if" it could give the legislator the power to enact the first Constitution, to turn the Constitution into a binding document.[105]

This approach can answer a famous critic to the notion of Basic Norm: that the whole positivist legal system will finally be built over a fiction. We defend here that the whole dynamic structure of legal power related to the normative creation is in fact founded on a fiction, but not the legal normative system, namely, the set of legal norms themselves. The searching for the justification of the validity of the norm can be retraced until the first Constitution of the Country, and the process stops there. Materially, there is no actual "material" legal element before the first Constitution – since the Basic Norm has no legal validity. We need the concept of Basic Norm only in a scientific level, as a presupposition in the mind of the jurist, as an intentional act towards the object of study, in order to give the system its unity and its legitimacy as a whole.

Also in philosophy, the topic of non-existence has a solid and long tradition, especially in the field of analytical philosophy. Even if the notion of existence

---

[105] We must remember that the first aim in using a fiction in science is always its practical utility. Loewenberg, J. (1912, p.717) explains clearly the notion of fiction according to Vaihinger's theory: "Fictions, in Vaihinger's usage, are not identical with figments, such as centaur or fairy, nor are they hypotheses capable of verification. They are deliberate devices (*Kunstgriffe*)on the part of thought for the practical purpose of successful orientation in and perfect control over the environment. Theoretically they are absolutely valueless. Applied with a knowledge of their fictitious character, they will lead to the intended practical results."

in philosophy is not the same as legal existence of validity, the fiction is also considered, in the philosophical domain, as a legitimate part of a theory and a useful scientific or epistemic device (also attested by the various and sometimes famous examples of *thought experiments* – which are also "as-if" kinds of construction – in philosophy). Surely we could also analyze those approaches to the question of non-existence, but none of them seem to really illustrate Kelsen's intentions with a notion such as the basic norm to the same extent that the philosophy of "as-if" proposed by Hans Vaihinger. It is, however, disappointing to notice the almost complete disregard to the writings of Vaihinger by the nowadays scientific and philosophical community. Nevertheless, this fact might be explained, even if it's not justified, by the original and unorthodox interpretations that Vaihinger has made concerning the works of Kant, as well as the severe skepticism derived from his view concerning fictions as being the only means to human epistemic access to the world.

So, going back to our topic and answering to the question from this section, the Basic Norm is definitely not a part of the legal system, but it is neither a part of the legal science. It is a presupposition from the jurist, precisely in the moment of his scientific consideration of the normative legal system as its object of study, being such a presupposition prior to any possible consideration about a specific legal system.

That will mean that, without conceiving the notion of Basic norm, without presupposing it in such a manner, no legal system can be rationally analyzed, studied or interpreted by a science. Without the fiction of a Basic Norm, the legal system will be just a multiple set of norms without inner cohesion, without beginning or end. The Basic Norm, according to our approach, should be seen as an inherent methodological procedure, prior to any consideration of a positive legal system, that is, the scientific approach towards any legal system must take into account the idea of the Basic Norm as the fiction necessary for the comprehension of the very object of the scientific study.

6.4 Final Remarks on this Topic

The fiction of the Basic Norm has to be clearly separated from the cases of legal fictions that we know since Roman law. The Basic Norm has no legal validity, has no regulating power in relation to our acts, it cannot even be formulated. In order to dissolve the confusion saying that Kelsen loses track in inserting a non-positive norm in its legal theory, we must understand that the Basic Norm is nothing more than a scientific methodological device, to be used only by the scientist. It has no direct relation with the ordinary norms of a system, it only works as a presupposition from the part of the jurist when it's question of considering a specific order as a whole valid and legitimate legal order.

In this perspective, it is legitimate to consider the Basic Norm as a tool or a device that allows the scientist to approach the legal system and, if we must make a metaphor here, we could borrow the beautiful image of Kant and say that the legal system can only be rationally regarded *through the lenses of the Basic Norm*.

The fictive character of the norm is explained by Kelsen's fascination with the work of Hans Vaihinger. Vaihinger's "philosophy of as-if" is perfectly adapted to what Kelsen wanted for the Basic Norm: to show that the use of a fiction in the frame of a science is perfectly viable in order to attain an objective that could not be attained otherwise: to give to the legal system the unity necessary to the legal analysis. To completely understand the necessity of the Basic Norm is to accept that it has to be completely separated from the legal system; it means to not be misled by the "norm" in Basic Norm.

When Kelsen adopted Vaihinger's "philosophy of as-if", he was certainly attracted by this notion of *"making* as-if" something were the case, and what we tried to clarify in this chapters the emphasis on the *"act"* of doing as if the Basic Norm existed. The Basic Norm is something that we *use*, it is a scientific *tool*. It is not a legal element and, if we stay strict, not even a methodological element, in the sense that it doesn't really make part of the legal science, but it must be a part, and it is an essential element, of the scientist's *approach* towards its objects, the legal norms. Without the presupposition of a Basic Norm by the jurist no theory can be founded, and no science can exist.

Chapter 7

Normative Conflicts and Temporality in Law

"Quod principi placuit legis habet vigorem."
Ulpianus

Normally, the main context giving rise to questions concerning the temporal aspect in Law are the ones involving cases of conflicting norms. To Kelsen, situations of norms in conflict must be solved not via the application of logical principles, namely by the principle of non-contradiction, and not even by traditional legal principles such as *lex posterior derogatpriori*, but rather by the application of a special kind of legal norm itself, to be called derogating norm.

The purpose of this chapter is to give an overall view of how norms relate to the temporal aspect in the frame of the kelsenian positivistic theory, namely how a norm "exists" in time, and how it can lose its validity over time. We will also analyze the question of retroactivity, and the question of the lacking of efficacy after a determined period of time and how it affects the losing of legal validity. Lastly, we aim to investigate how fictions, such as the Basic Norm, relate to time according to Kelsen's theory. All these elements will help us to better understand how central the temporal aspect is and how deeply it affects the legal validity in Kelsen's theory.

Before examining how the derogation works in cases of norms which might lose their validity in time or because of a situation of conflict, let us first analyze how normative validity relates to time in general.

7.1 **Norms *versus* Sentences**

It is never enough remaking that Kelsen's principal methodological interest is differentiating norms from sentences, as well as Law from Legal Science, and the problem he has in mind when doing so is the common practice (exemplified by the works of, among others, Walter Dubislav, Sigwart, Grue-Sörensen, Manfred Moritz or Ulrich Klug) of the application of logical principles to norms, mainly the inference rule in the context of normative creation, and the non-contradiction principle in the context of normative conflicts. Let us try to understand how the validity of norms can come to an ending or simply expire with time (something not to happen with the truthiness or falseness concerning sentences), and how Law dispose of special means to deal with this temporal aspect of normative validity.

The norm is expressed by an act which can be made explicit by various means, such as gestures, signs or imperatives. Norms are often expressed by imperatives, and don't have truth value: they can only be said to be valid. But they can also be described in sentences, like the ones which form the legal science, and those descriptions about norms can be true, if they affirm the fact of the validity of a norm, or false when the affirm the validity of a non-valid norm (or the contrary). In Kelsen's terminology, norms are said to be the sense of an act of will, meaning that they are valid when the behavior they display is the result of someone's (the Legislator's or the Judge's) willing.

In the same way, statements or sentences about norms are simply the sense of an act of thought, which can be evaluated as true or false as any other sentence.

The important point to us is that validity of norms and truth of sentences do not have the same temporal characteristics.

First of all, the main difference between the two is that norms are equivalent to validity, while the sentence displays the property of being true or false. The validity does not operate by giving a classification or qualification of a norm, in the same way that we can classify or qualify statements according to truth values, or at least that we can distinguish them according to their truth values. The norm is valid in the moment of its creation or, still, the norm is created already as a valid norm.

Then, in its creation, the norm is said to be valid for a determined space of time and territory, and this depends on the creator's willing. Differently, a true evaluated sentence, to Kelsen, possesses in itself the property of being true, independently of our knowledge about it. So, even if in the Middle Ages it was true to everybody that the Earth was the center of the universe, this was always and will always be a false sentence about it. It was our access to the real value of the sentence that was wrong. Similarly we can say that the statement affirming the heliocentric theory was not false (or incorrect) during the period of time regarding the middle Ages, but was and will always be a true or correct (except if one day in the future we discover that this information turns out to be wrong). Actually Kelsen is saying that a statement about a fact never alters its "original" truth value: it's the agent who either knows the truth value in question, either ignores it or makes a mistake concerning it.

Similarly, a false sentence is still considered to be a sentence, with the property or quality of expressing false information. It does not cease to be a sentence in the moment it is discovered to be transmitting false information. But the norm begins its existence from the moment on it obtains its validity, and ceases to exist in the moment when it loses it. That's why there can never be an invalid norm, because it would not be an existing norm. Valid norms exists – they are present in a legal order, their validity is fixed in time and space, they are positive – and invalid norms do not exist, they could not come into existence in the first place without the validity aspect.

Another interesting aspect concerning our problem consists in the fact that norms are not always expressed by conditionals or hypothetical ought-propositions, but rather by predictions, previsions or forecasts of a future event. So, when the norm is formulated saying that the guilty "will be" punished by such and such means, this does not mean the prediction of the application of the sanction, but it expresses, in a figure of speech, an imperative prescribing the application of the sanction. Even under those formulations, the norm does not predict the future, it has no informative sense, but prescriptive sense, and still can only be said to be valid.

Another relation between the validity and the temporal aspect is given via the notion of efficacy. So, the norm is valid once belonging to a legal order (via an act of will coming from an authorized person), but another condition is that this legal order must be, in its overall, also efficient.

So we can say that the efficacy of the order is a necessary (though not sufficient) condition for the validity of the norm. Hence, the efficacy is the direct link between the norm and the time/space aspect: by its efficacy we attest that the norm is observed or applied in reality, in the temporal, territorial, material and personal spheres, including its retroactive effect.

This last element leads to an important aspect of the temporal features of normative validity: the derogation.

7.2 Derogation

Besides commanding, permitting and authorizing, derogating is a specific function of the norm, with the specificity that it only takes place in relation to another norm's validity, which will be terminated by the derogating norm.

First of all, we must notice that it is not only via the "active" function of derogating, but also by the lacking of efficacy after a determined amount of time in which it has not being regularly applied that the norm loses its validity, that is, ceases to exist. In this case, the loss of the validity is explained by the lack of application of the norm during the time, and refers to the human behavior directly. Also, a norm can lose its validity by derogation simply when the authority understands that a determined norm is no longer desirable in the order. But the most common context of the derogation function is in cases of conflicting norms. We will come back to this special feature later[106].

7.2.1 *The Formulation of the Derogation Norm*

The derogating norm is not expressed by an imperative, simply because it does not prescribe a determined behavior or its abstention. The derogating

---

[106] Section 7.3 in this Chapter.

norm is always directed to another norm, which validity is about to be terminated. It assumes the form of an assertion of the kind: "The norm according to which X ought to Y is, by this means, repealed." Even if this assertion doesn't have an expressly prescriptive sense, it conserves its normative sense, for it is abolishing another norm's validity. Kelsen gives an example:

> "If there is a valid norm 'Males who are 21 years old and found fit for service are to do military service', and if the legislator were to posit the norm 'Males who are 21 years old and found fit for service are not to do military service', he would not repeal the validity of the first norm but posit a norm which conflicts with it. But a derogating norm does not conflict with the norm whose validity it repeals. But it is not possible linguistically to formulate the derogating norm in the following way: 'Males who are 21 years old and found fit for service not-are to do military service'. Hence derogating norms appear in the form of statements, for example, 'The validity of the norm 'Males etc.' is hereby repealed'. This statement does not have a descriptive but a prescriptive function, i. e., that of repealing the validity of a norm."[107]

Roman jurisprudence distinguishes between *abrogatio* as complete abolition from *derogatio* as partial annulation of a norm's validity. The complete abolition of a norm's validity refers to its substitution concerning for example another norm which the content will be more restricted concerning the territorial, temporal or personal aspect. As to the partial annulation, there is

---

[107] Kelsen, H. (1979, p. 108).

simply a change is the formulation of the normative content, which is not substituted by another norm, but reformulated with a slightly different content. We must note that Kelsen defends that, in the situation of normative conflict, one of the norms must be completely abolished; otherwise we would still be in presence of a conflicting situation. That's why, for Kelsen, the derogation is a specific normative function abolishing completely another norm's validity. Kelsen explains that:

> "The distinction between abrogare and derogare goes back to the celebrated passage in Cicero's Republic: 'It is a sin to try to alter (abrogare) this law, nor is it allowable to attempt to repeal (derogare) any part of it, and it is impossible to abolish (abrogare) it entirely' (iii.22). This passage clearly concerns a statute made up of many legal norms. But the principle Lex posterior derogat priori applies not only to the relations between statutes, but also to the relation between single legal norms, and in this principle the verb derogare means not only 'partial' repeal, but also 'total' repeal. I use the word 'derogation' in the sense of the repeal of the validity of a norm."[108]

7.3 The Context of Normative Conflict

---

[108] Kelsen, H. (1979, p. 114).

Normally, the derogation takes place when two norms are in conflict and then, either the validity of one norm is abolished and no new norm is created in its place, or a new norm is then created.

A situation of conflict between two norms means that obeying or applying one of the two implies, possibly or necessarily, infringing the other. But for the two norms to be in conflict, both of them need to be valid. And here we can see again the difference between norms and sentences: in the case of the norms, the derogation acts over one norm's validity which, from that moment on, ceases to exist; but in the case of the two contradictory sentences, one of the two is expressing something false from the beginning. Concerning the norms, even the descriptions of their validity are both true sentences, since the two norms are, by the time of the existence of the conflict, effectively valid.

The normative conflict can, but doesn't need to be solved by derogation, which is something to be stipulated by a legislative authority. The derogation is not a logical or legal principle, but a normative function, which can be executed also without the presence of conflict. But in the conflict situation, it is the case of a third norm directed to one of the conflicting norm's validity, in order to abolish it. This conflict can take place between norms of the same level, or between a norm superior and its inferior which were stipulated in different periods of time (one anterior and other posterior). Besides, the conflicting norms must belong to the one and the same normative order. So, if a moral norm is in conflict with a legal norm, the derogating norm coming from Law can only derogate the legal norm, and not the moral norm, and vice-versa.

7.3.1 *Some Examples*

According to Kelsen, the derogation as a normative function belongs not only to the legal domain, but also to positive Morals. Kelsen says:

> "It can also occur in a positive morality: for example, in Christian morality, when Jesus says: 'Ye have heard that it hath been said, Thou shalt love thy neighbor, and hate thine enemy. But I say unto you, Love your enemies...' (Matt. 5: 43-4). That means: I repeal the validity of the norm 'Hate your enemies' and I posit the norm 'Love your enemies'."[109]

But Kelsen also suggest that the most common in the Moral field is that a norm loses its validity not by an "active" procedure of derogation, but rather by the lacking of efficacy of this norm during time. On the legal field, one example that can be mentioned is the "Prohibition" concerning the manufacture and sale of alcohol during the 20th in the United States, and which has completely lost its efficacy at the point be formally repealed in 1933 by an official act: the 21st Amendment repealed the 18th Amendment to the US Constitution, by the method of the state ratifying convention.

Another interesting aspect concerns the Roman law principle called *lex superior derogat inferiori*, which is denied by Kelsen in its theory, since it is mistaken to think of one of the norms in conflict as derogating the validity of the other. The same thing happens concerning the context of conflicting norms from the same normative level, where Kelsen equally attacks the Roman law formula *lex porsteriori derogat priori*. Kelsen says that *"It does not also work as a principle the formula lex posteriori derogat priori, since*

---

[109] Kelsen, H. (1979, p. 106)

that it's not correct that the derogation comes from one of the conflicting norms. The derogation takes place only via the interpretation."[110]

Then, the reason why the formula *lex porterior derogat priori*as well as the formula *lex superior derogat inferiori* are mistaken is because they give the idea that the derogation is a function of one of the two norms in conflict. But those two norms are addressed to human behavior, not to normative validity. On the contrary, the derogating norm only exists in function of the norm to have its validity derogated: it comes into existence in the moment of conflict, in order to solve it, and ceases to exist once the conflict is solved and its function is performed.

Another reason why the formula of Roman jurisprudence *lex porterior derogat priori* is mistaken it's because it can be the first norm to be derogated, and also even both the conflicting norms. The derogating norm is presupposed by the authority in question, who assumes this norm in the moment of need, but it does not exist in the legal order among the other positive norms.

7.4 Retroactivity

When a norm is posited as valid, its validity concerns a determined territory and period of time, called the norm's *sphere of validity* (which by the way can also be unlimited). Concerning the temporal sphere, we must consider both the period of time before the norm is posited and after it. This could seem strange in the sense that, normally, a norm regards the regulation of the

---

[110] *Ibidem*, p. 236.

human behavior to take place after its existence, after the fact of being posited within a determined legal system. Nevertheless, it is still an open question if a norm can be also be directed to a behavior taking place before the existence of such a norm, and then we are talking about the norm's retroactive effect.

Most jurists will be against that legitimate existence of the retroactive effect of norms, to be accepted only, and still, maybe, if there is benefit for the defendant or when the law explicit indicates the effect.

These aspects are especially problematic when regarding cases of *ex post facto* laws regarding war crimes, for example, but also in the case of, for example, a statute of a regime becoming valid by a revolution which repeals the validity of the previous statute belonging to the substituted government. By the new statute, certain behaviors previously considered to be political crimes to be punished, will now be reconsidered. Kelsen says in a very clear manner that *"Admittedly, what is done cannot be undone, but the normative interpretation of events long past can be changed retroactively by means of norms posited after the events to be interpreted."*[111]

This is a complex matter and our intuitions indicate that Kelsen is mistaken in his approach to retroactivity. In the case of individual norms, they are indeed directed to a behavior which was performed before the enacting of the legal decision, but this does not indicate a retroactive effect, simply because this decision represents the application of a general norm already valid when the delictuous behavior took place. The legal decision only have retroactive effect when no general norm is applied, because there was no valid general norm concerning the case when in has occurred, i.e. if the behavior was not considered a delict by Law by the time it has occurred. But,

---

[111] Kelsen, H. (1979, p. 145).

as we have said, the retroactive effect is normally fully denied in most Countries, and Kelsen's inclination to it doesn't seem to be legitimate or defendable.

7.5 The Basic Norm

Now that we've seen how a positive norm's validity relates to the temporal aspect, let's see how this issue affects a normative fiction by excellence, which is in Kelsen's theory represented by the notion of Basic Norm.

According to Kelsen, there are norms which are not the meaning of an objective act of will, but merely the meaning of acts of thought. For example, I can think of a norm such as "All people are not to eat meat", but without wanting such a norm. The point is, nothing defends me though to think of this norm, even if it does not exists, if it is not a positive, binding norm on every people's behavior.

Kelsen's point is that, similarly to this case, there can be also norms that are the meaning of a fictitious act of will – they have a fictitious validity: we think of those norms *as if* they existed, *as if* they were valid, and one normally does that if there's some purpose or interest regarding the "existence" of such a norm.

As we have already seen, the notion of Basic Norm as a fiction is inserted in the discussion about the grounding of the legal positive order. In order to create a norm we need, first, of a more general norm with a correspondent content and, second, of an authority figure whose act of will will have the norm as its meaning. Given this context, one rapidly recognizes that the fact of going up in the normative hierarchy for the searching of the normative justification will lead us to the top of the normative pyramid illustrating the legal system. Then, what we will find on the top of it will have to be the Constitution, or, if we want to go even "higher", it will be the First Constitution of a Country. But, at that level, we are pushed to argue about what is giving the legitimating of the content of such a document and, even more, who could have given to the Legislator the authorization to elaborate such a binding document like the Constitution of a Country...

At this point Kelsen suggest that the only solution to this problem would be find if we presuppose a fictitious norm, which is not posited since this positing would again postpone the problem of the asking for the justification of such an existing norm as well as its author. Rather than this, we must simply make *as if* there were a norm higher than the Constitution, giving its legitimating. This presupposed higher norm would be the fictitious Basic Norm of each legal system.

Now, analyzing the relation of the Basic Norm's validity with the temporal aspect is a difficult issue, since the Basic Norm is not a valid norm. To be valid means to exist, to be posited, to be a part of the legal order. Rather, the Basic Norm is a thought norm, and we make as if it was valid. The Basic Norm is not even formulated, since to give content to it would mean having to justify it by a higher norm, which is exactly what we are trying to avoid. The great abstractive feature of this fake-norm detaches it from the spacious-temporal sphere.

In the present study we defend that, even if the Basic Norm cannot be recognized as a part of the legal system, it is not by so present in the legal system. We see the Basic Norm rather as a scientific tool, used by the legal scientist when is question to justify the legal order.

But concerning the temporal aspect of legal validity, it is still acceptable to think that, for example, every Constitution must be considered along with the idea of a fictive Basic Norm which justifies it (along with the whole legal system in consideration), and even that, if a Constitution is derogated, let's say because of a revolution, a new fiction of Basic Norm follows the new Constitution taking place. This perspective allows us to defend that the fictive validity of the Basic Norms will be as limited in time as the valid Constitution to which it is directed to scientifically justify.

7.6 Final Remarks on this Topic

With this exposition, our main objective was to situate the normative validity in relation to the temporal sphere. First, we analyzed the importance of differentiating valid norms from true/false sentences, and how both validity and truth values relate to time in different manners. Then we saw how the derogation is not a legal principle along with some Roman law formulas, but rather a normative function, having as main context situations of normative conflict. We also saw that the norms can lose their validity not via the derogation, but simply because of their lacking of efficacy over time. Afterwards, we studied how the normative retroactive effect, when admitted, affects the validity of norms and, at last, we saw that normative fictions do not relate to the temporal sphere in the same way as norms, since they do not have positive validity.

All these aspects show that the temporal sphere of validity plays a central role in Kelsen's legal theory. It helps us to better understand the particularities of the legal domain, and most of all it helps justifying Kelsen's worries in preserving the limits of Law from external elements, such as logical principles. In this sense, the specific relations between legal norms and the temporal aspect can then be seen as another evidence or another argument in favor of Kelsen's methodological "purity" of the legal theory.

Perhaps the main collaboration of this chapter was to show and explain that, since norms do not relate to their validity in the same way as sentences relate to their truth values, the situation of conflict cannot be compared to the situation of contradiction. This also represents the complete refusal of the possibility of application of the principle of non-contradiction to a situation of conflict between norms.

Chapter 8

The Notion of Practical Reasoning (Part I)

"Under normal conditions the research scientist is not an innovator but a solver of puzzles, and the puzzles upon which he concentrates are just those which he believes can be both stated and solved within the existing scientific tradition."
Thomas S. Kuhn

In this chapter 8 we propose to introduce the first part of a logical frame allowing us to display the argumentative features behind legal decisions and the justification provided by legal science. This undertaking is motivated by Hans Kelsen's solution to a well-known puzzle in legal philosophy, called Jørgensen's dilemma, based in the neutral element of the modally indifferent substrate.

In this Part I, we deliver a detailed presentation of the problem, as well as two of the many attempts to a solution. Then we present what we consider to be the final solution, given by the legal philosopher Hans Kelsen.

Based on this approach, the next chapter (Part II) will serve to introduce our attempts to provide, by means of a dialogical frame, an original application of the Kelsenian solution in the field of legal justification. This logical frame we propose not only perfectly displays Kelsen's approach but it also allows to express, debate and justify the legal reasoning without transgressing the limits between the legal field of normative creation and the scientific field of normative justification.

8.1 Introduction

The closeness between the domains of law and philosophy is corroborated by the prolific discussions concerning the foundations of the theory of law, namely the questions involving the definition of a legal norm. In a wide sense, norms are orders, commands deriving from human will; but legal norms specifically are obligatory imperatives, binding prescriptions, they are an "ought" (*Sollen*). According to Kelsen, there is a "methodological abyss", a gap between the "Ought" (*Sollen*) domain, where we find the norms, and the "Is" (*Sein*) domain, where we find the sentences, which are the result of an act of thought. Jorgensen's dilemma puts in question which kinds of interaction seem to prevail in the relation between prescriptions (*Sollsätze*) and descriptions (*Sätze*)[112].

This dilemma, as pointed out by Giovanni Sartor, "consists in the supposed necessity of making the following choice: Either one rejects using logic in the law (and more generally, in practical reasoning) or one has to admit that legal contents (practical noemata) can be true or false"[113]. In other words, the dilemma deals with the question whether imperatives can be a part of a logical inference, as one of the premises or as the conclusion. If a first

---

[112] This distinction will also be important in the differentiation between legal norms (*Rechts-Norm*) and normative propositions (*Rechts-Satz*).
[113] Cf. Sartor, G. (2005, p. 420).

reaction points to a negative answer (since norms cannot be true or false[114]), most of us will have to agree that inferences involving norms make part of our daily lives and that the evidence of their legal validity[115] seems to be out of question. This difficulty in understanding the role of imperatives in our reasoning about norms intrigued also Hans Kelsen, who severely criticized the answers previously given.

First of all, our aim is to explain how Kelsen deals with the dilemma, by arguing that there cannot be any logical derivation between imperatives (norms)and sentences. Then, we will show how Kelsen's approach offers a theoretical frame to a brand new treatment of problems like Jørgensen's dilemma and consequently helps us to provide an original answer to our first problem, namely: How can deontic logic be reconstructed in accord with the philosophical position that norms are neither true nor false?

In order to do so, we reconstruct the relations between law and legal science using a particular approach of logic, namely the dialogical approach[116]. Not only this framework allows us to respect the methodological abyss pointed out by Kelsen, but it also displays the interactions which are inherent to the legal reasoning. Our attempts are particularly directed to aspects concerning the justification of legal decisions, which will be in the following chapter considered within a logical frame, as a means to try to put in evidence the argumentative process involved in the legal reasoning.

---

[114] Norms are not facts, they are the "product" or the sense of an act of will, they are wanted by someone, and directed towards someone else's behavior.
[115] Here legal *validity* means the specific existence of a norm in a legal order. For a norm to be valid or existent in the legal order means that all the legal procedures to its creation were respected.
[116] Presented in the next chapter.

8.2 Understanding Jørgensen's Dilemma

Jørgensen's dilemma is inserted in the discussions concerning normative reasoning and deontic logic. It states the problematic fact that, even if it is commonly accepted that norms cannot receive logical treatment since they are not true or false, it seems to be legitimate to derive a specific norm from a general one, through a rational operation such as a syllogism. This syllogism should then be called "practical", because it contains norms as the major premise and as the conclusion.

The existence of practical syllogisms would affect many aspects of our understanding, dealing with questions going from the rationality of the normative discourse to the justification of moral acts and decisions, crossing controversial aspects such as the conflicts between norms, moral dilemmas and the possibility of a logic of norms.

8.3 First Attempts: Jørgensen and Ross

The easiest way to understand this problem, first announced by Jørgen Jørgensen in 1937, and named after this author by Alf Ross some years later (1944), is to immediately invoke some examples.

In our daily lives, we are frequently confronted with legal norms and imperatives in general, and we are demanded to ratiocinate and theorize about them. Most frequently, we do so without paying attention. Jørgensen's classical example is:

Keep your promises.

This is a promise of yours.
_____

Keep this promise.

The question imposed considers whether imperatives can be a part of a logical inference, as a premise or as the conclusion. Since norms cannot be true or false, it would seem reasonable to answer negatively. However, most of us will agree that practical syllogisms of the form of the example above seem to be legitimate, even if we have no criteria to distinguish valid practical syllogisms from invalid or arbitrary ones. This difficulty in understanding the role of imperatives in our reasoning about norms, commands, orders and in the legal argumentation was called by Alf Ross the "Jørgensen's Dilemma".

Let us analyze some examples given by Jørgen Jørgensen and Alf Ross, indicating the fact that the notion of practical syllogism is misleading and erroneous. Following a Kelsenian approach, the primal obstacle to the logical treatment of imperatives in a practical syllogism lies on the fact that they are not the objective sense of an act of will.

8.3.1 *Jørgensen's Answer to the Dilemma*

The main problem concerning Jørgensen's dilemma does not concern the fact of deriving norms from facts (or indicative sentences), but consists in logically derive a norm from another norm[117]. His first reaction to this problem is to say that imperatives (norms) cannot be a part of a syllogism,

___
[117] Cf. Cabrera, C. A. (1999, p. 207).

because they cannot be true or false. But then he proposes another approach to the logical treatment of those imperatives: Jorgensen says that the answer to the conundrum lays in the difference between the imperative factor and the indicative factor present in the norm.

Since there is no imperative without "something" which is demanded to be performed, there is always a possibility to detach the object of demand from the imperative. In this way, the *imperative* factor concerns the expression of the subject's state of mind: the act of commanding, the act of giving an order. The *indicative* factor concerns the specific content of the norm and has a propositional feature, and thus it may be treated with some logical tools[118].

In order to be able to logically manipulate the imperative we must, first of all, subtract the indicative factor from the imperative. So, from

"Tax evasion must be punished by fine and/or imprisonment"

we simply subtract the indicative sentence

"The norm demands that 'Tax evasion is punished by fine and/or imprisonment'"

and, in a simpler way, we can directly convert it to the indicative sentence

"Tax evasion is punished by fine and/or imprisonment"

which can then be evaluated as true/false. Now, since evidence shows that Jérôme C. actually practiced tax evasion, we are allowed derive another indicative sentence, namely,

"Jérôme C. is punished by fine and/or imprisonment".

---

[118] This form of distinction can be found later with the neustic/phrastic dichotomy in Hare (1972).

From that, we go the same way back by adding the imperative factor and reformulating a norm such as

"Jérôme C. must be punished by fine and/or imprisonment".

To Jørgensen, the translation procedure explains the efficacy of the practical syllogism, in the same way as it justifies the inference process. The syllogism is, according to him, legitimate, since, in fact, the inference is made concerning the indicative factor, and the norm is obtained by the reconstruction of the imperative factor.

8.3.2 Ross' Answer to the Dilemma

Ross severely criticizes Jørgensen's answer. The problem, says Ross, is that we are not able to reconstruct the norm "Jérôme C. must be punished by fine and/or imprisonment" (I2 in the figure below) from the first norm "Tax evasion must be punished by fine and/or imprisonment" (I1 in the figure below). Jørgensen's logic of satisfaction is useless to explain how we derive new norms as conclusions in the practical syllogisms[119]. In the figure below, Ross illustrates the gap through this illustration, where "I" stands for "Imperative" and "S" stands for "Sentence":

---

[119] Dependent on the efficacy of the norm. Ross explains: "[. . .] an imperative I1 is said to be satisfied when the corresponding indicative sentence S1 , describing the theme of demand, is true, and non- satisfied, when that sentence is false." See Ross, A. (1944, p. 37).

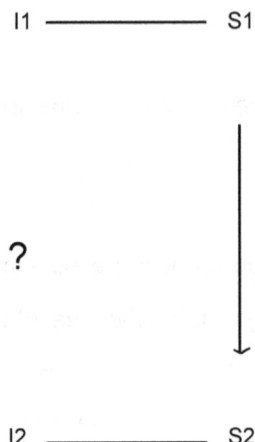

So, concerning the dilemma, even if Jørgensen says that we can logically approach the indicative factors of the norms involved in the practical syllogism, still there is nothing allowing him to say that we can derive a new imperative from the first one stated in the major premise, even if this procedure is made in an indirect manner. Therefore, the dilemma remains unsolved.

To solve Jørgensen's problem, Ross suggests several approaches. First, he suggest an alternative for the apofantic thesis that logic only deals with true/false valued sentences, by saying that the values true/false can be substituted by validity/invalidity, which now should be seen as the logical value of the norms but in a subjective way[120].

---

[120] We will analyze this misconception concerning the validity as a value of the imperative or norm later on this same section 8.3.2.

Ross understands validity as defined by "the presence of a state of mind in the person, that determines this validity", and depends on the will of the imperant. The validity turns into a psychological, not a semantic concept.

Ross starts his paper by stating the problem as being:

> "[. . .] to elucidate whether sentences which are not descriptive, but which express a demand, a wish, or the like, may be made objects of logical treatment in the same or a similar manner as the indicative sentences."[121]

Then, Ross proposes a wider delimitation of the logical domain, by suggesting the substitution of the logical values of truth and falsity by validity or invalidity. So, to fill up Jorgensen's gap in deriving I2 from I1 (See the next figure below), Ross declares the following:

> "It may then be laid down: if there be any sense in ascribing objective validity and invalidity to imperatives or to a certain group of imperatives, then it is possible to interpret the logical deductive system as being applicable to those imperatives. The logical deduction of I2 from I1 then means that I2 has objective validity in case I1 has objective validity."[122]

But how can we verify the validity/invalidity? Ross answers that the process of objective legitimating ignores the person and focuses only on the

---
[121] See Ross, A. (1944, p. 31).
[122] Ibid, p. 35.

impersonal norm, and this will finally lead to religious morals or to natural law kind of doctrines (imperatives without *imperator*).

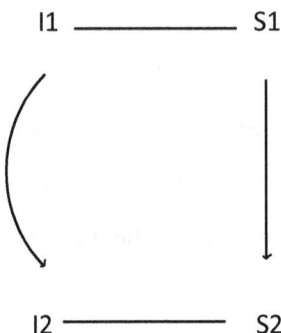

Then Ross considers a second possibility, saying that the means of verification of the validity lies on its satisfaction, so that we would have a perfect parallel between an imperative and its satisfaction. In this way, from the imperative "Close the door" we may have the correspondent sentence "The door is closed". Continuing the parallel, we must be capable of having also, for example, the negation of the sentence, i.e. "The door is not closed", from which we should attain the correspondent imperative "Don't close the door". So, in the inference, when we have "Close the door" satisfied, we must have also "The door is closed". Therefore, since the negation is false, its correspondent "Don't close the door" is not satisfied.

This example shows the complete lack of similarity between the prescriptive field and the logical field. Moreover, similarly to the negation, a disjunction could be added to the imperative, as in the famous example of "Slip the letter into the letter-box" to which we add the disjunction as: "Slip the letter into the letter-box or burn it". Even if the adding of the disjunction shows no problem concerning the truth values of the correspondent sentences, it is not evident, and even not plausible, that such a disjunction might be relevant in the normative domain, concerning the imperative form (the obligation of sending the letter doesn't imply the obligation of sending it and burning it—according to the inclusive disjunction—because the obligation of sending it is not satisfied if we burn the letter). These examples show precisely how deontic logic cannot grasp the relations between imperatives, and the analogy with the satisfaction is clearly not a good alternative.

Ross then finally proposes the third solution to the problem. The logical aspect of the imperatives in the practical inference concerns not the satisfaction or the verification, but the "subjective validity" of those imperatives. In this case, says Ross: *"An imperative I1 is said to be valid when a certain, further defined psychological state is present in a certain person, and to be non-valid when no such state is present."*[123]

The condition here is that the double validity/invalidity is defined by the truth/falsity of the corresponding indicative sentences, that is to say, the logic directly applied in the true/false valued sentences would be indirectly applied in the valid/non-valid imperatives when in presence of a determined psychological state. This new element would prevent us from the problems concerning the previous examples such as "Slip the letter in the letter-box or burn it!". The "psychological state" which Ross invokes would serve as a justification or a motivation to the imperant's will, avoiding trivialities. But this approach is doomed to refer always to a specific case (or a specific trial, for instance) where a norm or an imperative were applied regarding a specific case. Again, the normative relations are put aside, because it is the fact of the creation of the norm that is being asserted in a statement. As we will see next, according to Kelsen's approach, these kind of statements

---

[123] *Ibid.*, p. 38

actually compose the science of law, i.e. they are about the validity of the norm, for instance "There was enacted a valid norm saying that 'Murder is punished by imprisonment'", or "It is true that the norm 'X' was applied by Judge Z in case Y". Again, this can be logically treated (in the same way that legal science can be logically treated as any other science), but this does not take into account any relations between norms.

So, according to the transformations between imperative and indicative factors allowed by the rules of satisfaction, the validity of the first norm would be then preserved in the conclusion. But, since nothing guarantees that the person enacting the first order must also enact or want the specific order in the conclusion (in other words, there is no logical—nor legal— necessity between the two norms)[124], a psychological element is required. With this, Ross concludes that:

> "Imperatives can be constituent parts of genuine logical inferences, but if so, it is simply a question of a "translation" of logical inferences concerning indicative sentences about the psychological facts which define the "validity" of an imperative."[125]

So, Ross concludes that Jørgensen's dilemma is the result of a pseudo-logic puzzle. Even if Ross' approach is not restricted to the legal domain, but rather to the prescriptive domain in general, the problem of the legitimacy of the created norm remains the same. Besides, the author recognizes that he does

---

[124] The point here is that the specific norm in the conclusion depends on the act of will of the person enacting such a norm, and this process is not achieved through a syllogism. The judge can enact the particular norm without making use of the practical syllogism.
[125] *Ibid.*, p. 45.

not "solve" the puzzle, but rather shows that it is a pseudo-problem or, more precisely, the case of the use of some kind of pseudo-logic. He says that we simply consider as being a true evaluated statement the fact that a norm has been applied by a judge, and obeyed by a person, and the valid imperatives would be transformed in verifiable sentences such as "The judge X has enacted the norm 'Y'", or "This person has accepted the norm 'X'", which does not concern at all the prescriptive level anymore. It no longer represents a practical syllogism, because the norms are being simply described as having or having not taken place. That is why Ross calls it the application of pseudo-logic.

This discussion deals with many other situations of norm-creation, when the norm is enacted not by the judge or the legislator, but also by any other "authority", such as a father facing his son, or a teacher facing his/her students, or even cases of decision-making which could be reconstructed via a practical syllogism.

In the end, all these cases reflect a complete independence of the norm pretending to be the conclusion of the syllogism with respect to the norm admitted as a first premise. This correspondence has no effect on the preservation of the validity from the general norm in the premise to the specific norm in the conclusion. Or, in another words, the imperative in the conclusion is not legitimated or binding *because of* the departing imperative. And Ross himself recognizes that that is where the dilemma emerges: as the result of a psychological mistreatment of the norms.

8.4 Kelsen's Battle against the Dilemma

The works of Hans Kelsen are marked by the constant and close relation to philosophical questions, such as those involving normative justification. It is even a common saying in the juridical area that Kelsen was the greatest philosopher among the jurists and the greatest jurist among the philosophers of his time. So, the fact that he devoted a great deal of his attention to the problems concerning practical reasoning and more specifically to the Jørgensen's dilemma is not surprising.

In the next sections we will analyze how Kelsen treated the previous answers to this problem, and what was his particular solution to it. We must note that Kelsen's approach is marked by his principle concerning the existence of a methodological abyss between the domains of the "Ought" (the normative domain, formed by valid norms, accessed by acts of will—the domain of law) and the "Is" (the descriptive domain, formed by true/false sentences and descriptions, accessed by acts of thought—the domain of science). This conception is essential to understand how, similarly to Ross, Kelsen manages to show that Jørgensen's paradox is an illusion.

8.4.1 Correcting Jørgensen

To begin with Kelsen's treatment of Jørgensen's Dilemma, we must at first understand what this author means by the term "modally indifferent substrate".

When considering the differences between the norms ("ought" sentences) and descriptions of norms ("is" sentences), Kelsen insists on the fact that the two cannot be reducible or even comparable. One is the law, and the other is the science that describes the law as its object. Kelsen says:

> "'Is' and 'Ought' are purely formal concepts, two forms or modes which can assume any content whatsoever, but which must assume some content in order to be significant. It is something which is, and it is something which ought to be. But no specific content follows from the form."[126]

So, if we consider the following sentences:

1. "Jérôme C. ought to pay the taxes." and

2. "Jérôme C. pays/had paid his taxes."

We have one and only one modally indifferent substrate, which is "To pay the taxes", under two different modes, namely, the "ought" in 1. and the "is" in 2. Their content is identical, but the sentences themselves cannot be comparable, correspondent or deducible one from another.

So, concerning Jørgensen's solution to the dilemma, if we stick to Kelsen's conception of the modally indifferent substrate, we must notice that, in fact, the modally indifferent substrate is neither true nor false in itself. It can be the content of a sentence to be evaluated as true or false, in the same way that it can only be the content of a valid norm. But there is no correspondence between a true/false sentence and a valid norm; they only share the same modally indifferent substrate. So, when Jørgensen says that the answer to the dilemma is only a matter of translation, actually there is no correspondence between an imperative and an indicative sentence: the fact is that we are dealing with the same modally indifferent substrate,

---

[126] See Kelsen (1979, p. 58).

presented under two different modes. To sum up, the point of interest is that the modally indifferent substrate is outside the bounds of any logical approach.

8.4.2 *Correcting Ross*

As we have seen, Ross's approach takes as a point of departure the fact that the validity is the value of the norm (or of the imperative) in the same way that truth/falsity are the possible values of the indicative statement or a sentence. So, even if Ross's conclusion is that the dilemma is not legitimate since some pseudo-logic is being applied to the imperatives, all his argumentation lies in the presupposition that, when considering practical inferences, the validity is a value of the imperative in the same way that the truth is a value of the indicative statement. A nowadays critic will resume that: *"Ross directly attacks the idea that the validity, a specific quality of the prescriptive propositions, would be equivalent to the truth, a quality of the indicative propositions."*[127]

So, even if Ross' solution is closer to Kelsen extremism in denying the possibility of logical treatment of the norms, Ross takes the wrong way to arrive at this same conclusion[128].

---

[127] The original, in French: "Ross attaque directement l'idée selon laquelle la validité, qualité spécifique des propositions prescriptives, serait équivalente à la vérité, qualité des propositions indicatives." See Champeil- Desplats, V. (2002, p. 34).

[128] As we remember, Ross says that the logical treatment in a practical inference is an illusion, since the imperatives are actually treated as indicative statements (because the evaluation concerns the satisfaction of the norm, which is a verifiable fact).

Indeed, Kelsen will perfectly agree that they are not equivalent at all, but, more than that, Kelsen would also say that the validity is not even a value of the norm. Moreover, still about the differences between norms and statements, we must note that, when considering this cornerstone of Kelsen's legal theory, we immediately recognize that, actually, the validity can never be predicated from a norm in the same way that the truth is a property of a sentence to be evaluated as so. As we have already mentioned, the validity cannot be considered to be a property of the legal norm, because it is the very fact of the norm's pertinence to a legal system. The norm can only exist, it can only be considered as long as a valid norm. Moreover, while considering positive systems, this is the case for any normative system, including positive morals, and not only positive law.

Besides, as we ave also already explained, the main difference between a statement (*Satz*) and a norm (*Sollsatz*) is that the first is the result of an act of thought, and can be evaluated as true or false, and the second is the sense or the result of an act of will, and can only be valid. This main distinction allows Kelsen to give a more precise treatment than Ross with respect to the impossibility of deriving a binding imperative from a previous one: the "second" is the result of nothing but an act of will, whose sense is completely independent from the act of will giving place to the first norm or imperative. This leads Kelsen to explain that, even if the two imperatives display the same content (the same modally indifferent substrate), the acts of will must be two, neatly separated and independent from each other.

Before moving to the next section, it is important to note that it is clear from Ross' writings that he does not pretend to approach the practical syllogism from a legal perspective, as Kelsen does, but rather from the perspective of our daily situations of decision-making, or when confronted to imperatives in general. The problem, in this case, would not be the issue of the legal objective validity of the norm "obtained" in the conclusion of the practical syllogism, but rather its legitimacy, i.e. the fact of its abidingness given the first premise. The same question is posed in both approaches, namely, what renders this imperative in the conclusion obligatory or binding in relation to the first norm presented as a premise? Why do I, once having accepted the first imperative, must also obey the second?

8.4.3 *Kelsen's Final Solution*

So, after having seen Kelsen's position in front of the two answers given to the dilemma, how would Kelsen himself solve this puzzle? The answer lies in the difference between an act of thought and an act of will.

To Kelsen, every norm must have content, the "modally indifferent substrate", which is not the indicative factor as Jørgensen believed, but the behavior wanted by the *imperator*. So, in one way, the person enacting the norm knows the content of the norm, his will is directed to some behavior, indicated by the norm. On the other way, the addressee of the norm must also understand what is he supposed to do, how is he supposed to behave, and he does that by observing what is the content of the norm. Let us see how it works in an example. Consider the following case, a more extended version of the "Al Capone example" we mentioned when first introducing these differences.[129]

Every citizen should pay the taxes. This applies also to, let us say, the French citizen Jérôme C. Once a year he receives a letter saying how much he has to pay to the government, as income taxes. The legal norm behind the letter,

---

[129] Cf. chapter 5, section 5.2.

put in a simpler way, says that "Every citizen must pay his/her taxes", even if this very prescriptive element is not explicitly formulated in the text addressed to Jérôme C. The norm-positing subject can justify his demanding for the money by enumerating the benefits to be seized by the citizens, like the improvement of social and public services, the reduction of budget deficits, etc. In Kelsen's theory, those are to be seen as acts of thinking preceding the norm, and they have nothing to do with the will to have the taxes paid. They have nothing to do with the modally indifferent substrate, which is the behavior itself, in this case, "paying the taxes".

But let us see how Jérôme C. could be confronted to the imperative directed at him, namely "Every citizen must pay his/her taxes". Once confronted to this general norm (the first premise in the misleading "practical syllogism"), Jérôme C. can have acts of thought which allow him to understand what is he supposed to do, given his specific situation. He can think about things like "If a pay my taxes, my equals will benefit from the improvements in education, security, health care and so on". Also, he can consider that "If I don't pay the taxes, and if I figure out how to keep it secret, I can benefit myself from my own money. . . ". Outside the motivation frame, he must first of all understand that he is obliged to pay the taxes: the addressee of the norm must know what he is supposed to do. So, he also has acts of thinking which allow him to comprehend things like "it's me and no other person who has to pay these taxes", "I'm supposed to pay what it's said in the letter, not more nor less", and those are true/false evaluated statements, those are the sense of acts of thought. They don't belong to the norm in question; they are *about* the norm enacted. After understanding all that, Jérôme C. can accept that, once "Every citizen must pay his/her taxes" is valid (the sense of someone's act of will), and after the arriving of the letter from the tax collection, he must pay his taxes, i.e. he must perform himself the general norm which was, by the letters sent to him, applied to his case, understanding that "Jérôme C. must pay his taxes"—otherwise he will be in trouble. This concerns a fundamental division between thinking about possible norms, and wanting a norm, i.e. enacting it.

Concerning Jørgensen's approach, Kelsen says that the indicative factor pointed by this author has in fact a complete different meaning than the imperative factor. The indicative factor (the statement) is the outcome of an act of thought; the imperative factor (the command) is the sense of an act of will, and the two are completely independent from each other.

This is how Kelsen solves the dilemma. The misleading "practical syllogism" actually works in our daily lives because we are in fact reasoning about the norms involved in the inference, through acts of thought. It's natural that we try to understand what the norm is demanding, in order to know how to behave. The minor premise which poses a fact is actually the context in which we reason, and the major premise (indicating a norm in the practical syllogism) poses the norm that we must understand, comprehend, which presents the behavior wanted. If I understand the first premise in the context of the second premise, I'm able to know which behavior I'm supposed to have. All this procedure does not concern the normative level. Also, it's perfectly possible to understand the content of a general norm and not want to observe the behavior posed as obligatory. The particular norm posed as a conclusion in the practical syllogism will only be a legitimate valid norm after being also the meaning of an objective act of will.

8.5 Any Objections? Von Wright's Deontic Logic

When considering von Wright's first attempts to construct a logic of/for norms, we are confronted with definitions of the following type:

If an act is not permitted, it is called forbidden. For instance: Theft is not permitted, hence it is forbidden. We are *not allowed* to steal, hence we *must not* steal[130].

What von Wright tries to do is to use logical equivalence to establish the three deontic modes (obligatory, permitted and forbidden). In fact, given a primitive modality P (standing for "it's permitted that. . . ") and an arbitrary proposition ϕ, it is easy to define 1. a modality *forbidden* as $\neg P\phi$, i.e. it is not permitted that ϕ, so ϕ is forbidden, and 2. a modality *obligatory* as $\neg P\neg\phi$, i.e. it is not permitted that not ϕ, so ϕ is obligatory. This is exactly what von Wright does in his example: "forbidden" is equivalent to "not permitted". But Kelsen says that the only normative function is the mandatory function, norms have no permissive function. When von Wright says that "We ought to do that which we are not allowed not to do", he defines the obligatoriness of an act by the negation of the permission to not doing this act[131]. Norms start from the opposite, when something is commanded (mandatory normative function), the fact of abstention is qualified as not permitted. Everything we need is only the mandatory function, everything else is accessory.

Let us see what Kelsen himself says about it:

> "Wright says in this connection: 'If the negation of an act is forbidden, the act itself is called obligatory. For instance: it is forbidden to disobey the law, hence it is obligatory to obey the law' [. . .]. Since the normative function being considered

---
[130] See von Wright (1951, p. 3).
[131] See von Wright, G. H. (1951).

> is that of commanding, and since to forbid is to command an omission, things are being stood on their head when the being-commanded of an act is presented as the being-forbidden of its omission. 'It is commanded to obey the law': if we want to make use of the concept of forbidding, we can express the same idea by saying 'It is forbidden not to obey the law'. But things are back to front if we say 'It is forbidden not to obey the law, and hence it is commanded to obey the law'."[132]

Kelsen is right in saying that it seems strange to define what is obligatory by the negation of what is not permitted. But from a strictly logical point of view, if what is permitted can be defined by what is not obligatory, conversely, what is obligatory can be defined by what is not permitted not to do. It seems to be a tension between logical and legal interests. Moreover, in the introduction of von Wright's book[133], which includes a re-edition of "Deontic Logic", the author says that, about this last essay, a further refinement is needed in the treatment of this question:

> "Another application is to the logical study of the norms (normative discourse). This latter study is important to ethics and the philosophy of law. But it must be pursued with much more refinement than in my first paper (here republished) on deontic logic. Philosophically, I find this paper very unsatisfactory. For one thing, because it treats of norms as a kind of proposition which may be true or false. This, I think,

---

[132] See Kelsen, H. (1979, p. 322).
[133] See von Wright, G. H. (1957)

> is a mistake. Deontic logic gets part of its philosophic significance from the fact that norms and valuations, though removed from the realm of truth, yet are subject to logical law"[134].

This confession shows that von Wright actually commits the same mistake as his predecessors, Jørgensen and Ross. When he says that, even being "removed from the realm of truth", norm are still submitted to logic laws, he is actually stipulating some kind of strange correspondence between truth and legal validity.

8.6 Final Remarks on this Topic

In this chapter, we have just saw how Kelsen deals with problems derived from the falling into the naturalistic fallacy, such as Jørgensen's dilemma. As we also have seen, the means for the non-logical treatment of Jørgensen's dilemma lay on the notion of modally indifferent substrate, also highly dependent on the notions of act of thought and act of will, which we saw in detail in also the previous chapters.

Now, since we already know that it's not possible to treat the legal norms with principles of bivalent logic such as the principle of non-contradiction, the rule of inference, or the notion of practical syllogism, there's nevertheless another logical means to deal with this process.

---

[134] See von Wright, G. H. (1957, p. vii).

Whoever the candidate would be, it has to respect the methodological profile Kelsen draws for his legal theory. Besides, it is never enough to mention that any legitimate logical treatment of the legal field will be restricted to the scientific level, and not to a direct application to legal, moral norms or imperatives.

The methodological profile abovementioned will preserve the legal field from comparisons, translations or reductions to the indicative field, and rejects the insertion of truth values regarding norms. And that is simply because it is now attested that every approach that didn't observe those scientific precepts ended up failing in their purposes. In the next chapter of the present study, we will explain how such a prudent and cautious approach can render a coherent and relevant explanation of the process of legal creation and the justification of norms.

Chapter 9

The notion of Practical Reasoning (Part II)

> *"If we will disbelieve everything, because we cannot certainly know all things,*
> *we shall do much what as wisely as he who would not use his legs,*
> *but sit still and perish, because he had no wings to fly."*
> (John Locke)

Kelsen's approach to Jørgensen's dilemma gives us some insights about how to deal with the justification of legal decisions in the legal argumentation.

A legal decision involves a general norm that is applied by the judge in relation to a specific case (fact) in order to "create" a specific norm for that case. We all know now that the creation of a legal norm depends on an objective act of will coming from an authorized person, and no logical element interferes in this procedure. If we are about to deal with the normative reasoning (or the normative argumentation), the fact of trying to compare and correspond (legal) norms to (logical) propositions will forcedly lead to error. But with the notion of modally indifferent substrate, Kelsen shows that it is fairly possible to reason about norms, to evaluate our behavior in relation to a norm, without disrespecting the limits between these two domains.

This is precisely the purpose we pretend to develop in the present chapter[135]. We aim to show how is it possible to logically discuss and reason about norms, and still maintain the dichotomy between law and its science.

9.1 Dialogs about Kelsen's Solution

If we were to draw a scheme concerning the modally indifferent substrate (figure below), we must insist on the fact that this notion allows a double treatment of the normative content (the behavior "paying-taxes", as in our example) in terms of a (possibly) valid norm in the same way that it might assume a form of a sentence to be evaluated as true/false.

In the first case the dialogical approach to logic will deal with the normative construction in terms of a *Procedural justification*, while in the second case the treatment will be made in terms of a *Factual justification*[136]. The main point is that both the legal and the logical treatment respect and maintain the distinction between the two forms which can assume the same content.

---

[135] This chapter represents a cooperative work between the author of this book and Dr. Sébastien Magnier, who hereby receives also the expression of the author's full gratitude. This joint work is object of a publication. Cf. Sievers, J. & Magnier, S. (2015).

[136] See Section 9.3.2 in this Chapter.

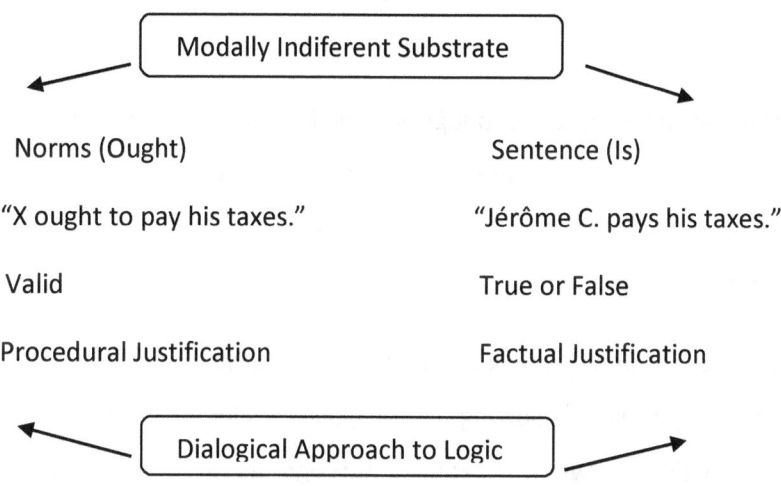

Regarding the process of normative creation, Jørgensen and Ross insist in considering the legal reasoning by forcedly comparing, corresponding, translating sentences into imperatives and vice-versa. In the end, this results in disturbing structures such as the practical syllogism. But once we have the legal material (namely, the norms used by the Judge and the facts), and if we then apply the (*dia*)logical approach to logic, it turns out that it's not only possible to deal with these two separated domains, but it's also possible to justify all the legal procedures by means of an argumentative process (as it is made in legal science).

This purpose does not aim towards a logical treatment of norms regarding the normative creation via logic, but it aims, rather, towards the logical analysis of the already created norms, i.e. of the sentences about their validity.

9.2 The Dialogical Approach to Logic

The dialogical approach to logic was first presented in the end of 1950's by Paul Lorenzen, and further developed by Kuno Lorenz[137]. During the 1990's, this kind of dialog was adapted and applied to different classical and non-classical logics[138].

The main idea of this approach is inspired by Wittgenstein's maxim of the "meaning as use". Following this idea, one can define a logical constant by its use made by two protagonists through an argumentative procedure. According to this argumentative procedure, a player proposes a thesis which he will have to defend against the other player, the latter being opposed to the thesis by trying to conceive a counter-argument. These two protagonists use the same rules, with one exception: the formal restriction[139]. This rule forbids Proponent to utter an atomic formula (i.e. a formula which does not contain logical connectives) if Opponent has not already uttered it. This restriction, in spite of its asymmetry, assures the logical truth, if Proponent manages to defend himself from anyone of his adversary's attacks[140]. This rule guarantees that Proponent's use of an atomic formula depends on a justification procedure, that is, the use of this atomic formula is independent of the notion of truth or falsity. Consequently, if Proponent wins[141], the thesis is a logical truth with respect to the dialogical system used. Moreover, during

---

[137] See Lorenzen and Lorenz (1978).
[138] This approach allows the combination and analysis of different logics in one and the same frame. See Rahman, S. (2006) for examples or Keiff, L. (2009) for a general view of these different developments.
[139] The overall set of used rules settles the dialog system. See. Appendix for a presentation of the standard rules of the dialogical approach to logic.
[140] Through the notion of winning strategy.
[141] See Winning Rule **SR-3**, Appendix, § Structural Rules for the definition of the principle regulating victory.

a dialog, a player can only attack the logical structure of his adversary's discourse, never the content of the discourse, nor even the adversary himself. If in this form of dialog the players commit themselves to defend their arguments announced during the play, those commitments are not about the content of the argument, but about their logical form. In other words, Opponent and Proponent are only committed to defend the logical structure of the propositions they use.

From a technical point of view, dialogic is not a specific logic, but rather a conceptual framework providing the study of different logics under an argumentative process. Dialogical language is defined from a determined logic where the letters **O** and **P**, standing for Opponent and Proponent, are added as well as the symbols "?" and "!". These symbols are required in the formulation of the rules of use of the logical constants: the *particle rules*. Another set of rules determine the conditions under which the particle rules have been or can be used. These are called the *structural rules*.

- *Modal Logic*

Modal Dialog results from an original idea coming from the researches of S. Rahman and H. Rückert[142]. This kind of dialog contextualizes the notion of proposition. If the standard dialog allows us to define the meaning of the logical constants through their use in an argumentative process, standard modal dialog allows us to associate a contextual dimension to this notion of use. The meaning of a logical constant is directly dependent on its contextual use. Not only the meaning is defined by its use, but this use is also dependent on a context. The context is then a constitutive part of the meaning of the

---

[142] See Rahman and Rückert (1999).

constant. Moreover, the pragmatic character of the dialogic semantics displays different interpretations of the modality simply by changing the associated structural rule. To our purposes, the modal operator receives a deontic interpretation, that is, we interpret the modal operator $O\phi$ as "it is obligatory that ϕ" or "ϕ ought to be the case".

9.2.1 *Dialog, Validity, Truth and Justification*

In this section we will present the formal details of our dialogs. But before that, we must explore both the advantages and inconvenient aspects of the dialogical approach concerning our problem, because if the dialogical frame allows an argumentative approach to logic, this frame is more concerned with the formal truth of a formula than its truth itself. This is the reason why we need some modifications of the standard dialogical framework.

The next paragraphs lay the groundwork for our conceptual modifications.

- *Material Dialog and Justification*

The dialogical approach to logic deals with the logical validity of a formula and not its truth value. But legal science, the discourse about the law, is evaluated in terms of truth rather than logical or legal validity. Besides, different approaches of the dialogic allow characterizing the truth value of a formula in *material dialog*[143].

---
[143] See Rahman and Tulenheimo (2009).

First of all, we need to consider initial concessions, i.e. some hypothesis over which the dialog will be constructed. Those hypotheses can be used by Proponent to justify his utterance. Thus, while in the dialogical approach we only consider Proponent's justification via the procedural use of atomic formulas, that is, we consider his saying: "I use this formula in the same context and in the same way you did", with material dialogs he can justify a proposition saying: "I use this proposition because it is an initial concession/premise". This tends to weaken the formal restriction: Proponent is no longer restricted by this rule, he can use the initial concessions to utter and/or justify his use of atomic propositions although Opponent has not already uttered them before.

- *Dialog about Truth*

From a logical point of view, material dialog deviates from the notion of winning strategy—which is, in dialogic, the counterpart notion of validity. With the material dialogs, a winning strategy for a given thesis becomes relative to a set of premises. It's only with regard to the set of premises that the winning strategy exists. So, it's possible to show that the thesis holds with respect to the premises given before the dialog, and this fits perfectly with the Kelsenian purpose saying that the legal theory is a true/false discourse raised from law.

Thus, even if this kind of dialog keeps us apart from the notion of logical validity, we stick to Hans Kelsen conception that the legal science only deals with truth.

- *Validity and Truth?*

According to Hans Kelsen, legal science – the discourse about the law – has to be supported by the law itself, i.e. a norm or a set of norms[144]. In the same way, the two players of the dialog discoursing about the law (about the normative creation or the legal decisions) have to support their arguments over this normative set and over what the Judge qualifies as facts according to a determined case[145].

In a given logical system a rule is not true nor false, but valid. A rule is valid inasmuch as it holds independently of its application. However, the particular application of this rule can be true or false, because it requires certain conditions to be fulfilled. If these conditions are not fulfilled, the rule cannot be applied, but this does not mean that the rule is invalid or false. The rule remains valid even when it's not the case that it has been or can be applied in the over mentioned circumstances[146].

In fact, the distinction between logical rule and particular proposition is analogous to the distinction between valid legal norm and contingent legal proposition. So, this distinction can be maintained and reconstructed if we distinguish two sets of premises: a set of general valid rules and a set of contingent propositions, each one of those representing, respectively, the set of norms and the set of facts.

- *Validity and Truth: a Difference concerning Justification.*

---

[144] The "Civil Code" or the "Constitution". See Kelsen, H. (1979, pp. 61-62 and pp. 81-82).

[145] Consequently, the corresponding dialog must beforehand suppose as admitted both the set of norms and a set of facts. This fits perfectly with the notion of initial concessions just mentioned.

[146] We will come back later to the discussion over validity and truth, with the justification notion.

Previously, we have put in evidence a crucial aspect, namely the incidence that a set of premises has in respect to the question of the justification of the atomic proposition. Standard dialogic limits itself to a procedural approach of the justification. It means that Proponent's use of an atomic proposition depends on a previous use of this proposition by Opponent. Implicitly, Proponent can justify its use by copying the procedure that Opponent could possibly follow to justify this proposition[147].

Material dialogs allow a justification for the use of an atomic proposition, but not due to its previous use by Opponent. Rather, the justification can be made because the proposition belongs to the set of initial concessions. Because of this authorization for this kind of justification, material dialogs are closer to the notion of truth and farther from the notion of validity. However, nothing prevents Proponent to use the procedural form of justification to justify an atomic proposition which do not belong to the set of initial concessions. In fact, it is possible to remove the formal restriction and to distinguish two distinct forms of justification: the procedural justification and the propositional justification. On one hand, the propositional justification allows to produce a justification with respect to truth, and on the other hand, the procedural justification has the same effects of the formal restriction and consequently preserves the (logical) validity level. The combination of these two kinds of justification in a same frame allows us to deal with the truth of a particular discourse and with the validity of a rule, without reducing the first to the latter and vice versa.

---

[147] Thanks to the justification rule that we introduce, this procedure becomes explicit.

9.3 The (Dia)logical Tools

We have chosen to benefit from the dialogical frame in order to maintain the distinction between law and legal science. But before developing these formal details, we have to specify first the dialogical modal frame under which our reflections are elaborated.

9.3.1 Preliminary Notions

With respect to standard propositional dialogic (presented in the Appendix), we have to add two operators in order to obtain a dynamic modal dialogic. The first operator corresponds to the modal operator O (previously mentioned in the Section 10.2, § Modal Dialogic). The second operator is the dynamic operator $[\phi]\psi$[148]. We interpret this operator as: "if ϕ is proved, then ψ holds"[149]. Whereas the introduction of a modal operator in a dialogical language demands the contextualization of the players' utterances, the dynamic operator prefixes the chosen contexts through a list A.

- *The Modal Operator O*

---

[148] Commonly known as the Public Announcement operator in Dynamic Epistemic Logic (DEL). See van Ditmarsch *et al.* (2008) for a DEL overview and Magnier, S. (2013), chap. 6-8), for more details about the juridical use of this dynamic operator.

[149] The dynamic operator entails a conditional form, but this conditional form is far from the well- known material conditional. The consequent requires that the antecedent is true. If the antecedent is not true, it cannot be announced and the consequent cannot be evaluated in the submodel where the antecedent was true before its announcement.

A contextual point is a positive integer labeling a formula[150]. The particle rule of the modal operator, presented in the table below, allows determining who between the challenger or the defendant will support the burden of the choice of the contextual point. With respect to our modal operator, the burden of the choice amounts to the challenger. Intuitively, this rule captures the following exchange: "if the player **X** utters, in the contextual point i, it is obligatory that ϕ, the player **Y** can choose a contextual point j in which **X** must defend that ϕ holds." The structural rule **SR-O**, displayed below, defines the conditions for the choice of the contextual point.

Burden and/or object Of choice	X-Utterance	Y-Challenge	X-Defence
O, the challenger chooses a contextual Point i^j	$A\|i:O\phi$	$A\|i:?_j$	$A\|i.j:\phi$

The modal Operator O

Structural rule **SR-O**:

To challenge a move $(O-A\|i...i^j:O\phi)$, P can choose any contextual point i^j already chosen by O.

The Dynamic Operator $[\phi]\psi$

In the particle rule as well as for the structural rule of the operator O, the contextual point i is prefixed by the list A. The necessity of this list appears in the particle rule of the dynamic operator and its associated structural rule.[151]

---

[150] A contextual point is not an atomic formula but it receives the same restriction, **P** only being capable of re-use those introduced by **O**.
[151] These rules are originally introduced in Magnier, S. (2011); soundness and completeness proof of them is given in Magnier and de Lima (2014).

The list A comes to enrich the notion of contextual point. Strictly speaking, it is not a new contextual point, it remains the same but prefixed by a list of ordered set of formulas. The list allows keeping track of the formulas coming from the dynamic operator[152].

Burden and/or object Of choice	X-Utterance	Y-Challenge	X-Defence
$[\phi]\psi$, the defender has the choice	$A\|i:[\phi]\psi$	$A\|i:?_{[]}$	$A\|i:\neg\phi$ or $A\bullet\phi\|i:\psi$

Because of the "if... then" form of this dynamic operator, the burden of the choice is supported by the defender. When the player Y challenges the evidence ϕ, X can reply "ϕ is not the case" or "because of the evidence ϕ, ψ is the case"[153].

The structural rule **SR-A** specifies certain conditions for the use of the list. The general idea of this rule is to ensure that a player who adds a formula in the list A is able to justify this formula[154].

---

[152] See Magnier, S. (2013, chap. 5).
[153] The dynamic operator $(\phi)\psi$, such that $(\phi)\psi \stackrel{def}{=} \neg[\phi]\neg\psi$, expresses the same idea but with a conjunctive form. So, in this case the burden of the choice is not supported by the defender but by the challenger.
[154] This rule is the counterpart of the fact that only true formulas can be used with this dynamic operator—what can sound a bit idealized if we consider evidence. An interesting point would be to consider refutable evidence, but to do this we need to use more sophisticated dynamic operators.

Structural rule SR-A:

> For any move $(X-\phi_1...\phi_n|i:e)$, player Y can compel X to utter the last element Φ_n of the list A:
>
> - In the contextual point i: $(Y-\phi_1...\phi_{n-1}|i:!_{(\phi_n)})$ or
> - in the contextual point j : $(Y-\phi_1...\phi_{n-1}|j:!_{(\phi_n)})$ife $=?_j$.

The rules presented above generate a dynamic modal dialogical frame. This dialogical frame allows evaluating the logical truth of modal dynamic formulas.

9.3.2 *Set of F Facts and the Problem of Justification*

In order to reach the truth level, we have to introduce the sets of premises called **N**orms and **F**acts[155] in the dialogical frame obtained, and re-found the question of justification of atomic formulas.

Definition 1 (Fact) *We take as a fact all data accepted by the Judge. These data are expressed by formulas in the set called **F**. This set is fixed before the dialog starts, and these formulas can be used in any contextual point of the dialog.*

---

[155] As discussed in Section "Validity and Truth?".

Those facts represent the data accepted by the Judge. For instance, in our example, "Jérôme C. has committed tax evasion" or "Jérôme C. has not committed tax evasion" are facts.

Recall: the two players can utter atomic formulas because we have eliminated the formal restriction. However, in order to maintain an internal coherence of the dialog, if a player uses an atomic formula, his adversary can compel him to justify it. That's why a justification rule is required.

The justification rule (**PR-J**) allows distinguishing between two different kinds of justification:

1. Propositional justification, and

2. Procedural justification[156].

This differentiates a justification which is based on the set of facts, from another which is founded in the argumentative process itself. It's possible for the latter kind of justification to not even be based on the facts[157]. A consequence of this is the fact that we need to add the following logical constant in our logical language:

[p] for all atomic propositions,

where [p] is a justification for the atomic proposition p.

- *1. Propositional Justification*

---

[156] Even if we present it in two distinct tables, it is in fact one and the same rule authorizing two different defenses.
[157] We come back to this distinction in the paragraph "Propositional and Procedural Justification".

A propositional justification can only be produced according to the set of facts F, i.e. an atomic proposition can only be propositionally justified if it belongs to the set F. This rule is described as the following:

Propositional justification	X-Utterance	Y-Challenge	X-Defence
A|i:p, the challenger requires a justification for proposition p.	A|i:p	A|i:!$_{[p]}$	A|i: [p]∈ F if p∈F

The set of facts (F) and the rule for the propositional justification allow establishing a perfect symmetry between Proponent and Opponent with respect to the moves they can make in the dialog. So, the two players have to use strictly the same rules[158].

- 2. Procedural Justification

In order to fully understand the rule of procedural justification, let us suppose that, during the play, player Y introduces an atomic proposition and, then, player X utters this same atomic proposition. Player Y can compel X to provide a justification for this atom. In this case, X can defend himself by copying Y's (possible) justification. That is possible only if this proposition belongs to Y's moves in the play, what we note as Y-moves (M/Y) in the rule displayed in the following table[159]:

---

[158] Normally, the two players do use the same rules, but the formal restriction introduces an asymmetry. Our justification rule allows establishing a strict and complete symmetry

[159] This rule gives a typical copycat procedure, i.e. a procedure identical to the formal restriction.

Procedural justification	X-Utterance	Y-Challenge	X-Defence
$A\|i{:}p$, the challenger requires a justification for the proposition p.	$A\|i{:}p$	$A\|i{:}!_{[p]}$	$A\|i{:}\ [p] \in M_Y$ if $\{A\|i{:}p\} \in$ Y-move

The procedural justification consists in justifying the uses that a player makes of an atomic proposition by a previous use made by his adversary in the game. Thus, when a player use this kind of justification, he affirms nothing more than "it's legitimate for me to use a proposition in the same conditions as you did".

- *Propositional and Procedural Justification*

While the propositional justification allows a link between an atomic proposition used in the dialog and its truth value fixed in the set of facts, the procedural justification allows us to use propositions that do not necessarily belong to the set of facts (**F**). The conditions of use of these propositions are identical for the two players. During the game, if a player introduces a new proposition, he authorizes his adversary to use this proposition under the same conditions and according to the same justification. Concerning the argumentative aspect, the main focus is not over the fact that a proposition belongs to the set **F** (consequently, over its truth value), but over the symmetry of the conditions of use of these propositions, i.e. whatever **X** does, **Y** can do the same.

Moreover, this strict symmetry between the two players let us consider the two players as having the same cognitive capacities (they can make the same inferences) and identical argumentative means (there is never imperfect or hidden information). From a strict juridical point of view, it would be difficult to consider an argumentative debate over law where the two protagonists won't have the same argumentative tools.

- *Factual Truth & Formal Truth*

The choice with respect to the nature of justification—propositional or procedural— is crucial because it permits to distinguish two levels of truth: factual truth and for- mal truth. On one hand, the propositional justification is based on the link between the propositions uttered during the dialog and the facts (admitted in *F*). Thus, this kind of justification allows us to establish a correspondence between the discourse and the facts, which is precisely the definition of truth. On the other hand, the procedural justification doesn't focus on the truth of discourse relatively to the facts.

Procedural justification is an internal form of justification, independent from the truth of the facts. It's based on the formal truth of the propositions, on the propositions' structure independently of their relation to the facts. This reveals a difference between the true propositions with respect to the facts, and the justifiable propositions with respect to a given procedure. If an atomic proposition belonging to the set *F* is necessarily true and can always be justified, the same doesn't happen with a justified atomic proposition, which is not therefore necessarily true. The procedural justification authorizes a justification independently of the propositional or factual truth.

The notion of justification is then founded over a larger notion than that of truth. It is founded over a player's ability to defend a proposition, so that a player can defend himself without using the truth notion. It's the player's use of the justification rule which finally determines the discourse level.

9.3.3 The **N** Normative System

Definition 2 (Norm) *For "Norm" we take the law used by a Judge and recognized as so by the two protagonists of the dialog. Those norms are formulated by general rules and constitute the set of norms **N**. This set is fixed before the beginning of the dialog and the general rules can be used in any contextual point of this dialog[160].*

A particular norm is produced from a more general one. This process passes by the Judge, who has a crucial role in the creation of the particular norm. He needs, on the one hand, to be based in the existence of a general norm with a corresponding content and, on the other hand, the particular fact concerning the affair in question. From that, once authorized by law itself, he is able to create a particular norm. According to Kelsen, a legal authority can fill up this role of creation of a particular norm. In the kind of dialogs we deal with, those general norms are reconstructed by the logical rules which determine the set **N**, i.e. the logical set of general rules should be seen as the counterpart of the legal set of general norms. These norms can be used by the players during the dialog, but under certain conditions, which arespecified in the following paragraphs. Before that, we have to mention a particularity concerning the use of the legal order in a dialog.

When a player wants to use one of the general norms of the set **N**, he expresses a *question* about the use of this general norm (which was used or could be used by the Judge). It cannot be a challenge against a previous move

---

[160]The set *N* cannot contain conflicting norms. This aspect is somewhat idealized, because it is not impossible for the norms to enter in conflict. The question concerning conflicts between norms and their choice is not of our interest by now, but could certainly be the object of future researches.

because players are not allowed to create particular norms, only the Judge is allowed to do this. So, the rule must be read in the following manner: "from a general norm belonging to the legal order, any player can ask his adversary if the Judge has used or could have use this norm to take his decision over an individual, which is represented in the rule by the choice of the individual constant *a*."

Rule for **N**

	N	Y-Question	X-Defence
(Ax→OBx) ∈N, Yasksif The norm can be applied to the Agent a.	A|i:Ax→OBx	A|i:?$_{a/x}$	A|i:Aa→OBa

In the formulation of the rule for the use of **N**, the predicates A and B are used to, respectively, designate an Act made by an agent *x* and a behavior to be imputed to the same agent *x* concerning this act. The "Ought" of this behavior is translated by the operator O presented in the Section 9.3.1.

- **N Normative System & its Conditions of Use**

If **Y**, in his question about the set **N**, can choose an individual constant, he is not therefore allowed to arbitrarily introduce a new individual constant in the play. The individual constant chosen must be previously given, i.e. at least one occurrence of the individual constant must occur in the play.

But the simple occurrence of the constant is not yet sufficient for the player to be able to request the set of norms. The antecedent of the demanded particular norm, containing the individual constant in question, must be a justified element in the list A. Thus, the particular norm $Aa \to OBa$ can only be obtained during the play if the defense for $[Aa]\psi$ leads the player to add Aa to the list A, that is, if there is an evidence that a satisfies the antecedent of the norm.

In fact, every justified proposition added to the list is called an evidence. But, since a proposition in the list A can be justified simply by its belonging to the set of facts **F** or, for those which do not belong, by the procedural justification, two kinds of evidence need to be distinguished:

1. $A \cap F$; and
2. $A \setminus F$.

The set $A \cap F$ describes the set of propositions belonging to the list A and to the set of facts, while $A \setminus F$ delimits the set of propositions belonging to the list A minus the propositions belonging to the set of facts. The justification of a proposition of the list by the set of facts (1) ensures that the demanded particular legal norm is created by the Judge with respect to the facts established and accepted by both players.

So, the Judge can create the particular norm because it is established that the act committed by a is a fact. If a general norm imputes a behavior B according to an act A, and if it's observed that, in the facts, the individual a has committed the act A, the Judge can create the particular norm imputing the behavior B for individual a.

However, for the propositions which do not belong to the set of facts (2), the justification can only be procedural. The subsequent evidence is not based on a veridical discourse (held by the notion of truth), but on the ability to defend by using the adversary's arguments. This warrants the validity of the

Judge's created norm, independently of his having recourse to the factual truth.

- *What is and What Could Have Been...*

The propositions in the list A depend on the players' ability to justify them. If we consider that the set F attributes a truth value to propositions belonging to it, propositions added to the list and justified using this set (propositional justification) describes *what is*, whereas propositions added to the list using the procedural justification represent *what could have been* or *could be* the case, but which is not the case with respect to the facts. From this, we can go on and distinguish two levels of discussion between Opponent and Proponent:

1. For all propositions verifying $A \cap F$, the players discuss about the particular norms created by the Judge with the established facts—the truth concerning the application of the particular norm with respect to the established facts.

2. For all propositions verifying $A \setminus F$, the players discuss about the particular norm that the Judge could have created or could create if the antecedent of the norm were/becomes an established fact—the validity of the general norm via the possible particularization independently of the facts.

From a strictly grammatical point of view, in the second level of the discussion, the question posed about the particular norm created by the Judge changes its mode. The first level of discourse corresponds to the indicative tense: there is a norm created by the Judge. The second level of discourse is performed under the past or present conditional tense: he could or could have created a norm such and such. . .

This changing of mode is interesting because it puts in evidence the conditional aspect of the normative creation regarding the existence of the fact. It is true that the general norm is formulated under a conditional proposition, but its use is itself conditioned by the existence of a fact corresponding to the normative antecedent. If the antecedent belongs to the set of facts, the grammatical mode is the indicative tense: Opponent and Proponent start the debate from the existence of a particular norm whose creation was linked to a fact. But, if the antecedent belongs to the list of announcements, but not to the set of facts, then the grammatical mode is the conditional tense. Opponent and Proponent consider the particular norm that could be or could have been created if the existence of the fact was or could someday be recognized. The procedure to follow is identical no matter whether the fact exists or not: the difference lies in the level of the mode and the justification. To the existing facts, it is the propositional justification which takes place (or the procedural justification, if the propositional justification was already used). To the non-existing facts, only the procedural justification can take place. So, the focus is not over the existence of the fact, but over the players' ability to justify their use of those facts. The players do "as if" the fact existed, even if it is not actually the case. In that case the fact is only used as an element inside a procedure.

The logical formalization which we introduced allows Opponent and Proponent to discourse about the particular norms created by the Judge, according to the facts and to the norms that could or could have been created if the existence of the fact was proven. In order to emphasize this distinction, we distinguish in the list what is justified by the set of facts from what can only be justified by a procedural means. For every proposition added to the list without being propositional justified (i.e. all proposition $\phi \in \{A \backslash F\}$), we add $*$, such that $\phi*$ means ϕ can only be procedural justified.

Thus, in a play, the propositions $\phi_1,... \phi_n$ in the list A have a truth value, while the proposition $\phi^*,... \phi^*$ have a value determined in terms of their capacity of being defended, i.e., a formal value.

9.4 The Dialogical System DLLC$_2$

We define the Dialogical Logic for Legal Condition **DLLC$_2$**:

Particle Rules = PR-SC $\cup$ PR-MO $\cup$ PR-DO $\cup$ PR-J ;
Structural Rules = SR-0 $\cup$ SR-1 $\cup$ SR-3 $\cup$ SR-O $\cup$ SR-A
These sets of rules must be used in a restrict dialogical frame, i.e. determined by the sets F and N. These two sets determine the conditions for the material dialog DM such that DM = F $\cup$ N.

Definition 3 (DLLC$_2$) *DLLC$_2$ is defined by the union of sets Particle Rules and Structural Rules used in DM:*

$$\frac{\text{DLLC2= PartRules} \cup \text{StrucRules}}{\text{DM}}$$

9.5 Jérôme C.'s Guilt and Further Discussions

Since the formal details are now presented, we can return to the example of the previous chapter and use those formal details to explore specifically our Jérôme C. example. Subsequently, we will discuss some properties of our dialogical frame underlined by the example.

9.5.1 Jérôme C.'s Example

In our Jérôme C.'s example we have used the norm "Tax evasion must be punished". We reconstruct this norm via the logical rule $Tx \to OPx$. Whereas the set N doesn't change, we do change the set F. Let us for now assume that "Jérôme C. has committed tax evasion" is a fact admitted by the Judge, as Tc (table below), and then let us consider that Tc is not admitted by the Judge and therefore does not belong to the set F (two following dialogs). As we will see, when Tc does not belong to the set F, the distinction between the two modes of discourse arises.

N
$Tx \to OPx$

F
Tc

Initial concessions for the dialog below

	O			P	
				$\varepsilon\|1:[T_c]OP_c$	0
	$m:=1$			$n:=2$	
1	$\varepsilon\|1:?_0$	0		$T_c\|1:OC_a$	2
3	$\varepsilon\|1:!_{(T_a)}$	2		$T_c\|1:P_c$	4
5	$\varepsilon\|1:!\ [T_a]$	4		$T_c\|1:[_c$	6
7	$T_c\|1:?_2$	2		$T_c\|1.2:P_c$	14
9	$T_c\|1:T_c \to OP_c$	N		$T_c\|1:?_{c/x}$	8
11	$T_c\|1:OP_c$	9		$T_c\|1:P_c$	10
13	$T_c\|1.2:P_c$	11		$T_c\|1:?_2$	12

Jérôme C. commits tax evasion

In the dialog above, Proponent adds Tc in the list A in move 2. In the next move, Opponent uses the structural rule **SR-A** to compel Proponent to utter this proposition in the contextual point 1, what he does in move 4. Then, Opponent requires a justification for the proposition Tc. Proponent manages to justify himself without difficulty, since Tc *belongs* to the set of facts (move 6). Once Tc *is* a fact belonging to the list of announcements, Proponent can request the legal order by asking for the particular norm created by the Judge with respect to fact Tc (move 8). Accordingly to this particular norm, Proponent manages to defend that it is true that Jérôme C. has committed tax evasion, and then it is obligatory that he has to be punished (move 14).

Now we consider what would happen if Tc is not an admitted fact.

Initial concessions for the next two dialogs below

	O			P	
				$\varepsilon\|1:[T_c]OP_c$	0
	m:=1			n:=2	
1	$\varepsilon\|1:?_{0}$	0		$\varepsilon\|1:\neg T_c$	2
3	$\varepsilon\|1:T_c$	2			
	−		3	$\varepsilon\|1:!_{[T_c]}$	4

Choice 1 – Indicative Tense

In the dialog above, Proponent chooses not to commit himself with the defense of Tc and he defends with ¬Aa. Opponent can then only challenge the negation (moves 2 – 3).

After this Opponent's challenge, Proponent has the choice:

1. He can require for a justification of Tc, or
2. He can use Opponent's challenge to change his previous defense.

In the table above we suppose that Proponent makes the choice 1. We develop the possibility of the choice 2. in the next dialog below.

Choice 1: After Opponent's move, Proponent requires a justification for Tc (move 4). Since Tc does not belong to the set **F**, Opponent cannot use the propositional justification. Unfortunately for Opponent, Tc does not belong to any Proponent's previous moves. So, he cannot use the procedural justification neither. Consequently, Opponent loses the play. Without proving Jérôme C.'s culpability, no particular norm could or could have been created by the Judge.

Choice 2: Opponent's challenge in move 3 allows Proponent to change his defense and then add Tc in the list A (move 4). Opponent uses the rule **SR-A** to compel Proponent to utter Tc in the contextual point 1 (moves 5-6). In the next move he requires a justification for Tc. Proponent cannot use the propositional justification, since Tc does not belong to F. Nevertheless (contrarily to the table considering Choice 1), the proposition Tc belongs to a previous move of Opponent. He had already uttered Tc when he challenged the negation (move 3). Regarding this move, Proponent has not required a justification, so he confers himself the possibility to reuse this proposition under the same conditions, and to justify it through a procedural justification. After this procedural justification, Tc gets marked by a * in the list, manifesting the change of mode of the discourse.

The progress of the play is then based on what would or could have been the case once Tc was an accepted fact. In move 10, Proponent asks for the particular norm that the Jude would or could have created if Tc was a fact. The rest of the play is similar to what is developed in the dialogue prior to this one, with the exception of the value of the players' discourse: they no longer debate over what is true, but rather over what could be or could have been true. The discourse is developed independently of the facts. It deals with the general norm's validity once its possible particularization, doing as if the fact was a verified and accepted one.

	O			P		
				$\varepsilon\|1:[T_c]OP_c$		0
	m:=1			n:=2		
1	$\varepsilon\|1:?_0$	0		$\varepsilon\|1:\neg T_c$		2
3	$\varepsilon\|1:T_c$	2		⊗		
				$T_c\|1:OP_c$		4
5	$\varepsilon\|1:!_{(T_c)}$	4		$T_c\|1:T_c$		6
7	$T_c\|1:!_{[T_c]}$	6		$T_c\|1:[\text{ }IEC$	o	8
9	$T_c^*\|1:?_2$	4		$T_c^*\|1.2:P_c$		16
11	$T_c^*\|1:T_c \rightarrow OP_c$	N		$T_c^*\|1:?_{c/x}$		10
13	$T_c^*\|1:OP_c$	11		$T_c^*\|1:T_c$		12
15	$T_c^*\|1.2:P_c$	13		$T_c^*\|1:?_2$		14

Choice 2 – Past or Present Conditional Tense

9.5.2 Further Discussions

The comparison between choices 1 and 2 has an important didactic aspect. Let us consider the object of the discussion between Proponent and Opponent:

Proponent presents the following argument: "if it is proven that Jérôme C. committed tax evasion, then the equivalent sanction ought to be applied". But, before entering in this discussion, Opponent and Proponent agree to recognize that it is not yet admitted that Jérôme C. committed tax evasion.

Consequently, Proponent only reaffirms that if Jérôme C. has committed tax evasion (which he is or could have been the suspect), it would be obligatory that he ought to be punished. The fact of his culpability does not change the fact of the obligation of the sanction in the case of culpability. Based on **F**, Proponent shows that it cannot be obligatory that Jérôme C. is punished if it is not established that he is guilty of tax evasion (table considering Choice 1). Using the procedural justification, it's reaffirmed the dependence between "being obligatory" and the satisfaction of the condition (i.e. the validity of the general norm). This aspect manifests the imputation aspect linking the condition (have committed tax evasion) to the "ought" element (the sanction: to punish the behavior). If the condition is not fulfilled, the "ought" concerning the behavior cannot take place. The tax evasion is the condition for the "ought", for the sanction, but the sanction is conditional because it rises from a modality. If the latter is not itself fulfilled, Proponent wins, but only because the conditional relation is not invalidated by the non-satisfaction of the condition. Thus, the norm remains valid independently of the fact that Jérôme C. has not committed tax evasion.

- *Back to the Evidence of the Illegal Act*

If the "ought" is associated with a condition, this condition has a particular character. It consists in the satisfaction of the particular norm's antecedent, what ensures the formulas added to the list *A*. Remember that these formulas have a particular status. When a player changes the situation of the argumentative process (by choosing a new contextual point), due to the rule **SR-A** his adversary can compel him to (re)utter and then (re)justify them in this chosen situation. Consequently, since a formula is introduced to the list *A*, a justification for this formula can be required in any new contextual point.

When players are incapable of producing this justification, the particular norm cannot be obtained in this contextual point. Hence the punishment could not be said to be obligatory in it.

In order to achieve the sanction, the guilt has not only to be a fact, but especially it must be proved, that's to say justified in any situation. It could not exist a situation in which the sanction is pronounced and where the guilt cannot be justified. Jérôme C. cannot be punished for a tax evasion that he has not really committed. But this doesn't mean that he should never be punished at all: only that, while in absence of a proof of his guilt, no sanction can be applied. Even if everybody knows that he is guilty, that's not sufficient for the sanction to have to be applied. It must be proven that Jérôme C. is guilty, and the formalism surrounding the dynamic operator explicitly allows this. Moreover, it remains possible for Jérôme C. to commit tax evasion without becoming a suspect of such an act. For this, it's enough that we cannot justify this fact in any situation.

For a sanction to be applied to a guilty behavior, we need that an authorized person (the Judge) creates a particular norm from a more general one, but also that this behavior is proven[161].

Remark: Deontic logic, in its treatment of legal norms, considers them as instantiations of general norms. The problem with this approach is that it reduces the normative propositions to conditional instantiations[162], what addresses deontic logic to paradoxes linked to the material conditional. In our reconstruction of the legal reasoning, our proposal also deals with the

---

[161] Even if the set F contains $\neg Tc$ or doesn't even contain Tc, identical plays will be produced. Maybe this indicates a link between the absence of the guilty proof and the innocence presumption.

[162] This is precisely the context where Jørgensen's dilemma emerges.

(material) conditional to formalize the general norms. But the use of those norms presupposes the creation of a particular norm (to be created by the Judge only).

The use of this particular norm is itself dependent on the evidence of the antecedent, which can only be attained by the dynamic operator. Thus, the obligation of the consequent is required only when the antecedent is true or procedurally justifiable. Consequently, due to this formalization, not only the falsity of the antecedent cannot lead to the trivialization of the conditional relation, but also it allows us to study the meaning of a norm through its description, in order to give the conditions of its use when the fact is missing (procedural justification) or to give the truth conditions of the particular norm if the fact is the case (propositional justification).

9.6. Back to Jørgensen's Dilemma and Final Remarks

This original dialogical approach to logic is the most relevant frame to display the process concerning normative creation through an argumentative practice. We respect and preserve all the Kelsenian theses with respect to the dualisms between the realm of "Is" and the realm of "Ought", between law and its science or theory, between a norm and its description, between the "legal actor"—the Judge, the Legislator, the authorized person—and the persons external to the legal procedures—the jurist, the legal scientist. All those elements play a specific role in our study of the legal reasoning through the process of a dialog, and they are essential to show how mistaken is the notion of a practical syllogism, which lead to theoretical problems like Jørgensen's dilemma.

Regarding the dilemma, Kelsen had pointed out the fact that to create a particular norm (in the conclusion of Jorgensen's practical syllogism) the creator has to have the power to do so. In the legal context, this power, this authorization, must come from the law. Legal norms are always created via procedures which are internal to law itself. No one from the outside is able to create a valid norm, even with the support of the existence of a more general norm with the correspondent content. This is a necessary, but not sufficient, step in the normative creation. The "authorization" aspect cannot be ignored, and can never be attained by someone who is outside from the legal sphere. Each one of us, as citizens, is able to put a norm in question, to evaluate it as fair or unfair, to consider if it should be or not applied to a determined case. But Kelsen emphasizes that those are all acts of thought that do not attain the legal level of the valid act of will, which could be produced by anyone but the Judge, or the authorized person.

With the dialogs, what happens is a procedure of justification after this act of will has taken place in time. Moreover, it is a procedure which allows considering what would be the case once other conditions were at stake. Proponent and Opponent have no legal authority, they only discuss about the legal procedure, once it has already been achieved. Certainly, this can clear up a lot of legal aspects such as mistakes or flaws to be revealed in the process, and that is all the interest of a legal theory.

This approach fits perfectly with Kelsen's solution to Jørgensen's dilemma, saying that we are all capable of questioning, justifying and reasoning about norms.

We can guess what would be the result (the conclusion on the misleading practical reasoning), i.e. what would "normally" be the content of the result of a legal decision, for example. But by no means are we able to state this "result" as being a valid norm. There is no way to trespass the inference barrier in the practical syllogism, because there is no such a way for a syllogism to be a practical one: syllogisms are constructed by acts of thought, and practical decisions are made by acts of will. It is a mistake to accept that we can simply mix up the two, or translate one into another, as it is a mistake to consider that norms can result of acts of thinking.

Finally, we believe that our dialogic approach shows a perfect example of an application of Kelsen's theory concerning the important question of the normative creation. It displays how it is possible to confront oneself to general norms like "Tax evasion must be punished" and particular norms like "Jérôme C. (who committed tax evasion) must be punished" from a completely external point of view, and the justification element is central in this undertaking.

We preserve Kelsen's temperance about the modally indifferent substrate, yet showing how far we can still go in analyzing the different possibilities of interpretation. We show that it is perfectly acceptable to analyze, theorize, argue, examine, debate about norms, without transgressing the limits between the normative (practical) and the descriptive (theoretical) levels, and still preserving the methodological principle of "purity". From this cautious and solid methodological approach, no harming puzzles arise.

Chapter 10

Final Remarks

The present book represents a real effort towards testing the limits of approximation between the fields of Law and Philosophy. This undertaking is justified by the fact we expect have made clear that, despite refusing the possibility of applying logical principles such as the principle of non-contradiction and the rules of inference directly to the legal field, Kelsen seems more enthusiastic regarding a dialog between the two disciplines when the notions coming from the philosophical field serve to the legal science as a means to approach its objects, namely, the legal norms.

Let us then make a recapitulation of the contents explored in the present work.

As we stated in the Introduction, our purpose with the present work was to investigate the stability of the possible relations between the fields of Philosophy and Law. Since our context of analysis is the legal theory proposed by Hans Kelsen, this purpose is undertaken by taking as background the traditional problem of the possibility of the application of logical principles to norms.

This application was a widespread practice regarding Kelsen's contemporary colleagues, while his view on the issue was always marked by a strong skepticism. Thus, while the general practice in legal theory seemed to take for granted the identification of legal norms with true sentences, Kelsen's writings grew more and more explicit concerning his negative perspective of the approximation between the fields of Law and Logic.

The originality of our approach consists in showing, as explicitly as possible, that the rejection of Kelsen concerning the relations between Law and Philosophy is not so straightforward, even – and, we dare to say: especially – in the last work, the *General Theory of Norms*, where Kelsen meticulously express by all means the differences between the indicative and the prescriptive domains.

We defend that Kelsen's treatment of the problems involving that relation is complex. The thesis we tried to defend points to the fact that, while the direct application of logical principles to norms is expressly denied, the use of some methodological principles and concepts belonging originally to the philosophical field are encouraged for the work of the legal scientist, in his task of describing, interpreting and justifying the intra-relations of the normative system. Those concepts are mainly represented by the naturalistic fallacy and the fiction as a methodological tool, and the philosophy authors praised by Kelsen are represented, mostly, by Immanuel Kant, David Hume and Hans Vaihinger.

We also analyzed the alternatives that Kelsen offers when rejecting the logical principles, such as the case of derogation as an alternative to the principle of non-contradiction, and the notion of modally indifferent substrate as a means to understand the process of normative creation without making reference to the rule of inference or to structures such as the misleading practical syllogism.

Other than that, we offered our own attempt to logically formalize the legal procedure of justification of the normative creation, which we intend to have presented as a legitimate instantiation of the Kelsenian theses of preservation of the methodological principles guaranteeing and attesting the "purity" of Law.

In order to better recognize and corroborate each one of the contributions we provide for the question of the relations between philosophy and the legal field as it is considered by the positivist tradition, let us now analyze, one by one, each of the chapters composing the present study.

In chapter 2, *"The Author and his Theory"*, we tried to provide the context and the motivation that pushed Hans Kelsen to develop his scientific theory for the study of positive legal orders. We explained the difference between legal positivism and the alternative schools of thought like the legal realism and the natural law tradition. This comparison was useful to make clear why the frame of the positivist tradition was chosen by Kelsen for his project of a "pure" theory of law, which preserves the autonomy of the normative field concerning, for example, other disciplines, such as sociology or religious oriented moral approaches.

Concerning Kelsen's works, we explained the fact of the differences between his approach in the *Pure Theory of Law* with respect to his later work, the *General Theory of Norms*, especially regarding the question of the possible relations between law and logic. We also gave a general overview of the academic life of Kelsen, from his first works in Vienna until his later departure to the United States.

In chapter 3, *"Preliminary Notions"*, we offer a wide overview of the main notions composing Kelsen's special terminology for his legal theory. We start with the notion of legal validity, with its particular meaning of normative existence. Once knowing that validity equals to the existence of a norm, and defining the legal norm as the objective meaning of an act of will, we explained how those norms relate to the science describing them, and the importance of not falling into the naturalistic fallacy.

Then, we discussed the formulation of the positive norm, and how the norm is not a simple imperative, because of its binding force. Regarding the normative construction based in conditional or hypothetical norms, we also remarked the differences between causality and imputation. Since those notions form a "conceptual web", we are able to inter-relate them, noticing that, for example, concerning the dichotomy of causality/imputation, it is in fact directly linked to the division between science and its object, which is by its turn regulated by the methodological abyss between "Is" and "Ought", which should be kept separated from each other in order to avoid the falling into the naturalistic fallacy...

Still in this rather long chapter, we also took a glimpse at the notion of fiction in the context of legal positivism. This notion was introduced when we first explained the construction of the normative system according to a hierarchical structure, having at the top of it the problematic notion of basic norm as a fiction, regulating and authorizing the creation of the legal norms of the system

Then, we approached the two main questions dealt by Kelsen in the *General Theory of Norms*. The first is the possibility of the application of the principle of non-contradiction in the case of conflicting norms. Kelsen denies this possibility, by making reference to the notion of derogation as a legitimate legal means to deal with the conflict. The second is the possibility of the application of the rule of inference in the case of normative creation. This procedure would be expressed by the practical syllogism, representing the use of the practical resoning in order to obtain a new norm in the conclusion. Once again, Kelsen will deny this possibility, by attacking all and every comparison or identification of the valid norm with a truth-valued sentence.

After this general terminological background, we were able to finally approach the specific questions concerning the relations between law and philosophy, one by one, as well as giving our contribution to the treatment of the different topics.

So, in chapter 4, "*Legal Positivism: A Defense of the Scientific Method*", we tried to collaborate in the discussion concerning the historical antagonism between the currents of legal positivism and natural law. After explaining to a greater extent the reasons for the hostility regarding the defenders of each of those approaches, we heed the fact that it would still be perfectly possible to build a scientific approach to morality as far as it consist in positive morality.

That remark is based on the division between static and dynamic principles operating in the intra-normative relations. Actually, the last work of Kelsen intends to be a theory for norms in general. Besides, most of the examples Kelsen uses to illustrate his thesis, not only in the *Ganeral Theory of Norms,* are examples coming from positive religion. We defend the view that the positivism *qua* method of knowledge of a given set of norms is capable to report also norms involving non-scientific notions in their content, i.e., to attest their validity as posited norms forming a system ruled by a static principle. This aspect may represent a softening of the tensions involving the two kinds of approach.

In chapter 5, *"Science and Method: The Naturalistic Fallacy"*, the relations between the fields of philosophy and law were finally tighten, when Kelsen recognizes many similarities in David Hume's skeptical and above all fundamentally empirical approach to the knowledge of a determined scientific object. Kelsen recognized the precepts of the legal positivistic perspective in Hume's conceptions, especially concerning the method of scientific approach, which seems to fit perfectly to Kelsen's "purist" ideal. We analyze and reinforce the closeness between Hume's and Kelsen's approaches.

Chapter 6, called *"The Non-Existence in Legal Science"*, we dealt with another very philosophical subject, that of non-existence, which was developed and studied by means of the notion of fiction. Again, as he have done concerning the philosophy of David Hume, Kelsen grounds his approach in the notion of fiction proposed in the "philosophy of the as-if" of the German philosopher Hans Vaihinger.

Kelsen's interest is on presenting the notion of basic norm as a fictional methodological device allowing the comprehension of the legal system as an object of knowledge. We believe to have offered a clear survey in favor of that perspective, by explaining the purely methodological use (rather than a prescriptive function) of the notion of fiction as a scientific tool to deal with the problem of justification, and insisting that the appeals for the fiction is made only by the jurist in the precise moment of having to face the legal system as a cognoscible object. Our original approach concerns the attempting to the fact that, in the same way as the basic norm is not placed in the legal system together with the other norms, it is also not placed in the scientific level as a scientific principle. We insisted in the notion of basic norm as a presupposition during the specific *act* of the scientist when he is confronted to the problems of legal grounding.

In chapter 7, "*Normative Conflicts and Temporality in Law*", the Kelsenian view concerning the notions coming from the philosophical (or logical) field and directed to the legal field shifts to a very negative one. Actually, Kelsen is simply remaining loyal to the idea that logic or philosophy cannot be applied directly to the legal norms, but only to legal science as a means to facilitate and help to approach the law. So, when in this chapter we analyze the problem of conflicts of norms, Kelsen says that the application of the principle of non-contradiction consists in a methodological error, because that principle presupposes the existence of truth values, which cannot be attributed to legal norms.

Instead, Kelsen introduced the notion of derogation as a normative function destined to deal with the cases of normative conflict. In the same way, we have also analyzed the use of derogation in cases other than the conflict, namely the cases of lost of efficacy over time.

The purpose here was to make explicit the selection concerning the admissions Kelsen seems to be ready to approve regarding the logical/philosophical elements in the field of law. Since the case of the application of the principle of non-contradiction represents an attempt to actually trespass the methodological abyss, by performing the principle's "function" inside the normative level, by treating norms as if they had truth values just like the sentences of the indicative mode, Kelsen is categorical concerning the refusal of any possibility concerning that application.

The same happens in chapter 8, "*The Notion of Practical Reasoning (Part I)*", concerning the rule of inference in the context of normative creation. The admission of this rule would be normally expressed in structures such as the practical syllogism, for example, where valid norms and true sentences are identically regarded and treated by traditional bivalent logic. The point is that, even if most examples of practical inferences seem to be, intuitively, evidently valid, there is nevertheless no means to legitimate those arguments.

This interesting puzzling aspect was remarked by Jørgensen and named after him by Alf Ross as the "Jørgensen dilemma". In this chapter we have studied how Kelsen criticized the answers that were offered by Jørgensen himself and also, later, by Ross concerning the dilemma. Then we analyze Kelsen's own answer to the dilemma, based on the important notion of modally indifferent substrate.

The notion of modally indifferent substrate can be seen as the main answer Kelsen gives to the overall attempts in applying logic to norms. An this is because of the fact that this notion must be understood as being itself the actual content of the legal norm, a neutral element that can assume either the indicative or the prescriptive forms, but that in itself has no value whatsoever: it is impartial, indifferent. The consequences on the adoption of such a notion in the context of legal positivism is the ultimate refusal of any identification between sentences and norms, since they represent simple the two modes where the modally indifferent substrate may be inserted, but without having to establish any relation between the modes themselves.

In this manner, after introducing the notion of modally indifferent substrate, we proceed, in the chapter 9, called *"The Notion of Practical Reasoning (Part II)"*, to an attempt towards a legitimate formalization of the process of normative creation once it has already happened in time, as well as the justification of that juridical process. In order to succeed in such attempt, we use the dialogical approach to logic to display the process of normative creation without infringing either the methodological "abyss" between normative and indicative fields, neither the principle of "purity" so cherished by Hans Kelsen. More than that, we intend to have collaborated to the building of solid relations between the legal and the philosophical (or logical) fields, based on the solid methodological ground that is expected concerning the Kelsenian approach of legal norms.

This last chapter, where we have provided our attempts towards a formalization of some legal processes without logically "affecting" the normative level, and thereby still preserving the so appreciated notion of methodological "purity", might also be a first step towards further possible developments in the legitimate and conscious approximations between the domains of logic and law. We hope the present work has offered the solid basis and a clear background for such future undertakings.

Appendix

Propositional Dialogic in a Nutshell

This appendix present the rules of Propositional Dialogic, i. e., the particle rules for the propositional connectors $\neg, \wedge, \vee, \rightarrow$ and the standard structural rules.

How should the particle rules be read?

The reading of the particle rules is straightforward once we keep in mind the notion of usage of the logical constant that they represent. A particle rule can be decrypted via these three points[163]:

1. an **X**'s utterance,

2. a challenge, which is the demanding made by player **Y** over the initial **X**'s utterance,

3. a defense, corresponding to the answer of player **X** to the challenge made by **Y**.

---

[163] Except for the rule for negation since there is no defense.

Burden and/or object Of choice	X-Utterance	Y-Challenge	X-defenced eX
¬, there is no defence	$A\|i:\neg\phi$	$A\|i:\phi$	⊗
∧, the challenger has the choice	$A\|i:\phi\wedge\psi$	$A\|i:?_{\wedge1}$ or $A\|i:?_{\wedge2}$	$A\|i:\phi$ respectively $A\|i:\psi$
∨, the defender has the choice	$A\|i:\phi\vee\psi$	$A\|i:?_{\vee}$	$A\|i:\phi$ or $A\|i:\psi$
→, both players shared The burden	$A\|i:\psi\rightarrow\phi$	$A\|i:\psi$	$A\|i:\phi$

Standard connectives – **PR-SC**

Particle Rules

Before presenting the structural rules, we have to deliver one more definition: that of repetition rank. A repetition rank is a positive integer corresponding to the number of times that a player can repeat the same challenge or the same defense[164].

Structural Rules

Starting-Rule SR-0: Any play $d\Delta$ of a dialog $D\Delta$ starts with **P** uttering Δ — the thesis. After the utterance of the thesis, **O** has to choose a repetition rank. **P** chooses his repetition rank right after **O**.

Playing-Rule SR-1: Players move alternatively. Each following the repetition rank is either a challenge or a defense concerning a previous challenge.

---

[164] See Clerbout (2013, chap. 2) for a further discussion on repetition ranks.

Atomic Restriction SR-2: **P** cannot utter an atomic formula first. He is only allowed to re-use those previously uttered by **O**.

Winning-Rule SR-3: A player **X** wins a play if and only if it is **Y**'s turn play but he cannot move anymore with respect to the rules.

Bibliography

Aquinas, T. (2014). Summa Theologiae I-II qq. 90-106.The Summa Theologica: Complete Edition. Catholic Way Publishing. New York. [1265–1274].

Aristotle. Rethoric. Book 1: Chapter 13. [1373b]

Austin, J. (1995). The Province of Jurisprudence Determined. W. Rumble (Eds.).Cambridge University Press. Cambridge [1832].

Bindreiter, U. (2002). Why Grundnorm? A treatise on the Implications of Kelsen's Doctrine. In:*Kluwer Law International*. Law and Philosophy Library. Neatherlands.

Bobbio, N. (2008). Direito e Poder.Translation of Nilson Moulin. Ed. UNESP. São Paulo.

Bobbio, N. (1997).Teoría General del Derecho. Editorial Temis. Santa Fé de Bogotá, Colômbia.

Bulygin, E. (1990). An Antinomy in Kelsen's Pure Theory of Law. In: *Ratio Juris*, 3. Pp. 29-45.

Cabrera, C. A. (1999). Imperativos y lógica en Jørgen Jørgensen. In: *Isegoría*, 20. Pp. 207–215.

Calhoun, G. C. (1944) Xenophon, Memorabilia, I. ii. 40-6, trans. George C. Calhoun. In: *Calhoun, Introduction to Greek Legal Science* (Oxford: Clarendon Press, 1944, repr. Scientia: Aalen, [1977]).

Celano, B. (2000). Kelsen's Concept of the Authority of Law. In: *Law and Philosophy*, Vol. 19, No. 2, Mar, p. 173-199.

Champeil-Desplats, V. (2002). Alf Ross: droit et logique. In : *Droit et société*, (1). Pp. 29–42.

Clerbout, N. (2013). Étude de quelques sémantiques dialogiques. Concepts fondamentaux et éléments de métathéorie. PhD Thesis, Université de Lille.

Curry, O. (2006). Who's Afraid of the Naturalistic Fallacy? In: *Evolutionary Psychology*, 4. Pp. 234-247.

Beyleveld, D.& Brownsword, R. (1998). Methodological Syncretism in Kelsen's Pure Theory of Law. In: *Norms and Normativity*. Stanley and Bonnie Paulson (Eds.).Clarendon Press Oxford.

Gabbay, D. & Woods, J. (2010). Logic and the Law: Crossing the Lines of Discipline. In: *Approaches to Legal Rationality*. Gabbay, Canivez, Rahman, Thiercelin (Eds.). Logic, Epistemolog, and the Unity of Science. Volume 20. Springer.

Hansen, J., Pigozzi, G. and van der Torre, L. (2007). Ten philosophical problems in deontic logic. In: Proceedings of Normative Multi-agent Systems, NORMAS 2007.

Hare, R. M. (1972). The language of morals. Oxford University Press. Oxford.

Hart, H. (1998). Kelsen visited. In: *Norms and Normativity*. Paulson, S. & Paulson, B. (Eds.). Clarendon Press Oxford, p. 70.

Hart, H. (1983). Kelsen Visited. In: *Essays in Jurisprudence and Philosophy*. Oxford: Clarendon Press, 286-308.

Heidemann, C. (1997). Die Norm als Tatsache: Zur Normentheorie Hans Kelsens. Baden-Baden. Nomos.

Holmes, O.W. (1881). The Common Law. Available at: http://www.gutenberg.org/files/2449/2449-h/2449-h.html

Hume, D. (2007). A Treatise of Human Nature. Reprinted from the Original Edition in three volumes by L.A. Selby-Bigge, M.A. Oxford: Clarendon Press. [1739].

Kammerhofer, J. (2005). Unearthing Structural Uncertainty through Neo-Kelsenian Consistency: Conflicts of Norms in International Law. In: *Papers of the European Society of International Law*. December 2005.

Kant, I. (2005). Groundwork of the Metaphysics of Morals. Routledge, New York. [1785].

Kant, I. (1998). *Critique of Pure Reason*. Cambridge University Press. Cambridge. [1781].

Keiff, L. (2009). Dialogical logic. http://plato.stanford.edu/entries/

Kelsen, H. (1923). *Hauptprobleme der Staatsrechtslehre*. 2nd printing (Tübingen: J. C. B. Mohr).

Kelsen (1960). Pure Theory of Law. Translated from the German by Max Knight. University of California Press, 1989.

Kelsen, H. (1979). General Theory of Norms. Clarendon Press, Oxford, 2001.

Kelsen, H. (1998). The Pure Theory of Law, 'Labandism' and Neo-Kantism. A Letter to Renato Treves. In: *Norms and Normativity*. Paulson, S. & Paulson, B. (Eds.). Clarendon Press Oxford, p.169-175.

Kelsen, H. (2008). What is Justice? Justice, Law and Politics in the Mirror of Science. Collected Essays. University of California Press, Berkeley, Los Angeles [1957]. Repr. The Lawbook Exchange, Clark, New Jersey.

Loewenberg, J. (1912). Review. In: The Journal of Philosophy, Psychology and Scientific Methods, Vol. 9, No. 26 (Dec. 19, 1912).

Lorenzen, P. and Lorenz, K. (1978). *Dialogische Logik*. Wissenschaftliche Buchgesellschaft, Darm- Stadt.

Magnier, S. (2012). PAC vs. DEMAL, A Dialogical Reconstruction of Public Announcement Logic with Common Knowledge. In:*Logic of Knowledge.*

Theory and Applications.C. Barès, S. Magnier, and F. Salguero (Eds.). College Publications, London. Pp. 159–179.

Magnier, S. (2013). *Approche dialogique de la dynamique épistémique et de la condition juridique*. College Publications, London.

Magnier, S. &de Lima, T. (2014). A Soundness & Completeness Proof on Dialogs and Dynamic Epistemic Logic. P. Allo, F. Poggiolesi, and S. Smets (Eds.). In: *Dynamics in Logic*. Logique et Analyse.

Mangier, S. & Rahman, S. (2012). Leibniz's Notion of Conditional Right and the Dynamics of Public Announcement. In:*Limits of knowledge society*, D.G. Sambotin (Ed.), pp. 87-103.

Natural Law for Today's Lawyer. In: *Stanford Law Review*, Vol. 9, No. 3, May, 1957, p. 479.

Ott, W. (1987). Bericht von einem Besuch bei Prof. H.L.A. Hart in Oxford. Duncker &Humblot. Berlin.

Paulson, S. (1992). 'The Neo-Kantian Dimension of Kelsen's Pure Theory of Law'. In: *Oxford Journal of Legal Studies*, 12. Oxford University Press.

Paulson, S. (1998). Four Phases in Hans Kelsen's Legal Theory? Reflections on a Periodization. In: *Oxford Journal of Legal Studies*, 18. Oxford University Press. Pp. 153-166.

Paulson, S. (1999). Arriving at a Defensible Periodization of Hans Kelsen's Legal Theory. In: *Oxford Journal of Legal Studies*, 19. Oxford University Press. Pp. 351-364.

Pfersmann, O. (2004). Les modes de la fiction. Droit et littérature. In : *Usages et théories de la fiction, Le débat contemporain à l'épreuve des textes anciens*. Françoise Lavocat (Dir.). Rennes, Presses Universitaires de Rennes. Pp. 39-61.

Poincaré, H. (1982). The Foundations of Science: Science and Hypothesis, The Value of Science, Science and Method. University Press of America. [1913].

Rahman, S. (2006). Non-normal dialogics for a wonderful world and more. In:*The Age of AlternativeLogics*. Pp. 311–334.

Rahman, S. & Rückert, H. (1999). Dialogische Modallogik (für T, B, S4, und S5). In: *Logique et Analyse*, 167(168). Pp. 243–282.

Rahman S. & Tulenheimo, T. (2009). From games to dialogues and back. In: *Games: Unifying Logic, Language, and Philosophy*. Pp. 153–208.

Reynolds, B. (1993).Natural Law versus Positivism: The Fundamental Conflict. In: *Oxford Journal of Legal Studies*. Vol. 13, No. 4, Winter.

Ross, A. (1944). Imperatives and logic. In:*Philosophy of Science*, 11(1). Pp. 30–46.

Ross, A. (1961). Validity and the Conflict between Legal Positivism and Natural Law. In: *Revista Juridica de Buenos Aires*, n°4. Pp. 46-93.

Sartor, G. (2005). Legal Reasoning: A Cognitive Approach to the Law. In: *Treatise on LegalPhilosophy and General Jurisprudence*, Vol. 5. Springer, Berlin.

Shapiro, S. J. (2009). What is the Rule of Recognition (And does it Exist)? In: *Public Law & Legal Theory Research Paper Series*. Research Paper No. 181. YALE Law School.

Sievers, J. (2009). "Kelsen sobre o Lugar da Lógica no Âmbito Normativo. (Master's Dissertation).
Available at: http://w3.ufsm.br/ppgf/menuesp2/404d5d77d7e8468e2c0e3fafa65fdb4f.pdf

Sievers, J. (2011). Peut-on respecter une norme impossible? In : *Normes et Fiction*. Cahiers de Logique et Epistemologie. College Publications. London, pp. 123-140.

Sievers, J. & Rahman, S. (2011). Normes et Fiction. Cahiers de Logique et Epistemologie. College Publications. London.

Sievers, J. & Magnier, S. (2015). Reasoning with Form and Content. In: *Past and Present Interactions in Legal Reasoning and Logic*. Armgardt, M., Canivez, P. & Chassagnard-Pinet, S. (Eds.). Logic, Argumentation & Reasoning, Vol. 7. Springer.

Silving, H. (1955). The Twilight Zone of Positive and Natural Law. In: *California Law Review*, Vol. 43, No. 3, Jul., p. 489.

Spaak, T. (2005). "Kelsen and Hart on the Normativity of Law". In: *Perspectives on Jurisprudence: Essays in Honour of Jes Bjarup*. Peter Wahlgren (Ed.). Pp. 397-414.

Student Author (2002). Lessons from Abroad: Mathematical, Poetic, and Literary Fictions in the Law. In: *Harvard Law Review*.Vol. 115, No. 8 (Jun., 2002). Pp. 2228-2249.

Styron, W. (1987). Sophie's Choice. Corgi, London [1979].

Vaihinger, H. (1911).*The Philosophy of "As-If": a system of the theoretical, practical and religious fictions of mankind*. London, Routledge & K. Paul, 1965.

van Ditmarsch, H., van der Hoek, W. and Kooi, B. (2008). *Dynamic Epistemic Logic*. In: *Synthese Library: Studies in Epistemology, Logic, Methodology, and Philosophy of Science*. 337. Springer, Dordrecht.

van Roermund, B. (2000). "Authority and Authorization". In: *Law and Philosophy*, Springer, Vol. 19, No. 2. Pp. 201-222.

von Wright, G. H. (1951) Deontic logic. In:*Mind*, 60(237). Pp. 1–15.

von Wright, G. H. (1957). Logical studies. Routledge and K. Paul, London.

Winkel, L. (2004). Peace Treaties and International Law in European History. Randall Lesaffer (Ed.). Cambridge University Press.

Wolfe, C. (2003). Understanding Natural Law. In: *The Good Society*. Penn State University Press, Vol. 12, No. 3.

Wood, N. (1988). Cicero's Social and Political Thought. University of California Press. Berkeley and Los Angeles, California.

Xenophon, Memorabilia, I. ii. 40-6, trans. George C. Calhoun. In: *Calhoun, Introduction to Greek Legal Science* (Oxford: Clarendon Press, 1944, repr. Scientia: Aalen, 1977), Pp. 78-80.

www.ingramcontent.com/pod-product-compliance
Lightning Source LLC
Chambersburg PA
CBHW071606170426
43196CB00033B/2105